THE FOUNDING OF
THE T'ANG DYNASTY
THE FALL OF SUI AND RISE OF T'ANG

AMERICAN COUNCIL OF LEARNED SOCIETIES

STUDIES IN CHINESE AND RELATED CIVILIZATIONS

NUMBER 4

The series of which this volume is a part is published through the generosity of the late MARGARET WATSON PARKER, *of Detroit, who wished thus to honor the memory of* CHARLES JAMES MORSE, *a pioneer collector and student of the things Oriental, but who, during her lifetime, preferred that her gift remain anonymous.*

EMPEROR KAO-TSU OF THE T'ANG DYNASTY

A portrait by Wei Wu-t'ien 韋無忝, formerly in the Palace Museum at Peip'ing. From a photograph in the collection of Dr. John C. Ferguson.

THE FOUNDING
OF THE T'ANG DYNASTY

THE FALL OF SUI AND RISE OF T'ANG
A PRELIMINARY SURVEY

BY

WOODBRIDGE BINGHAM

OCTAGON BOOKS

A DIVISION OF FARRAR, STRAUS AND GIROUX

New York   1975

Copyright, 1941
by The American Council of Learned Societies

Reprinted 1970
by special arrangement with The American Council of Learned Societies

Second Octagon printing 1975

OCTAGON BOOKS
A DIVISION OF FARRAR, STRAUS & GIROUX, INC.
19 Union Square West
New York, N.Y. 10003

.

LIBRARY OF CONGRESS CATALOG CARD NUMBER: 75-115965
ISBN 0-374-90635-1
9-19-79

Printed in USA by
Thomson-Shore, Inc.
Dexter, Michigan

TO MY FATHER

From whom I derived my earliest
inspiration for historical study

TABLE OF CONTENTS

MAPS
    I. The Sui empire about 610
  IIa. Central and North China: Spread of banditry and
       rebellion, 613–617 (to Ta-yeh 13th year, 5th moon)
  IIb. Central and North China in 617

PREFACE

Chinese internal history of the middle periods, including the great T'ang and Sung dynasties, has hitherto received little serious attention among western scholars. In this respect the early seventh century is a typical example. A comprehensive outline of events based on a study of the sources is not yet available. Only a few reliable translations and monographs have appeared in western languages and the excellent material presented in them has been largely confined to certain special topics.[1]

In what way does this small and remote section of human history merit further research? Why should one attempt to fill in this particular gap in our knowledge? The answer may be given in two ways.

The end of the sixth century and the first years of the seventh marked the beginning of the "Golden Age" of the Sui and T'ang periods. After centuries of political disruption during which China had been invaded from the north and west and had been greatly affected by outside influences, chiefly Buddhism, the country was reunited under the Sui dynasty, 589–618. The latter year saw the beginning of the T'ang dynasty, an age of vigorous empire, which produced some of the world's greatest poetry and art, and which evolved a political and administrative system that was to be the model for future empires in the centuries to come.

Among the statesmen who inaugurated an age of such broad accomplishments was one whose formative years coincided with the early decades of the seventh century,—the second T'ang Emperor, Li Shih-min, known to history as T'ai-tsung. He grew up during the latter years of the Sui rule and became prominent in the founding of a new dynasty. He played a conspicuous part in the political and cultural developments of his time and has since become one of the outstanding figures in the

1. See the works of Chavannes, Des Rotours, Jäger, and others listed in the Bibliography.

history of the Far East. For a knowledge of this great emperor and the T'ang period as a whole it is essential to understand what happened at the time of change from one dynasty to the other.

What was the political situation in China at the end of the Sui period which prevented that dynasty, after having unified the country, from being the one to endure? And how, among the many contenders for imperial power who again temporarily split up China into several hostile divisions, were Li Yüan, Duke of T'ang, and his son Li Shih-min so well able to take the lead and to succeed when others failed?

In this study the primary effort has been directed towards determining the chronological sequence of events as given in the basic annals of the four dynastic histories covering this period: the *Sui History* (or *Book of Sui*), the *Northern History*, and the *Old* and *New T'ang Histories*.[2] Research has not, however, been confined to these brief skeletal accounts of events. Reference has also been made to the biographies and monographs contained in these dynastic histories and to other contemporary sources.

Some of these sources, in particular the *Court Journal of the Founding of the Great T'ang* by Wên Ta-ya,[3] deserve much fuller study than has been given them in this preliminary survey, and the author intends that they will form the basis for more extended research on the beginnings of the T'ang dynasty.

To aid in clarifying the subject supplementary tables on chronology, genealogy, and official titles, together with three maps and a descriptive note concerning these maps, have been appended to this monograph.

Events in the Chinese texts are dated according to the ancient lunar calendar. These dates have been changed to their European equivalents and are thus given in the body of the narrative, or, in the case of the many rebellions at the end of the Sui, in Appendix D. The original Chinese dates have been inserted in the footnotes in order to facilitate ready reference to the texts. A brief chronological correspondence table, Appendix A, has been

2. See Bibliography, Nos. 8, 9, 10 and 11.
3. See Bibliography, No. 12.

included. In the Chinese calendar important events are dated according to the days of the moon or lunar month and also according to a cycle of sixty terms which is used in dates quite independently of the days of the moon. Its use is comparable to that of the seven-day week in the west. In the sources the cyclical terms are usually employed, and accordingly their sequence has been generally indicated in the footnotes. All dates identified by one number only are those of the sexagenary cycle, unless specifically mentioned otherwise. Numbers are used for cyclical dates, both in the text and the appendices, as the equivalents of the Chinese characters. Hence the form "13th year, 5th moon, day 16" is intended to show that such a day is the day *chi mao*,[4] the sixteenth day of the sexagenary cycle, and not the sixteenth day of the moon. When, as in a few instances, the form "16th day" is used it represents the day of the moon.

Biographical dates, given in the genealogical table, Appendix B, and after the Chinese characters in the footnotes, are for brevity presented only in western form. They have been determined in most cases by reference to the dynastic annals and the biographies noted.

Chinese names and other words whose transliteration has been included are romanized according to the Wade system of Giles's *Chinese-English Dictionary*, with the exception of certain place names, such as Foochow, Yangtze, and Shansi, for which another transcription has become well established. Old regional names (not always used in the same sense today), such as Ho-nan, Shantung and Kuan-chung, have been translated throughout this work. The English forms, though cumbersome, may help in clarifying the location of events. Names of the Korean states are transliterated according to the McCune-Reischauer system of romanization.[5]

4. 已卯. These cyclical characters may be most easily found in Herbert A. Giles, *A Chinese-English Dictionary* (2nd edition, London, 1912), Part I, p. 32, Table L.

5. George M. McCune and Edwin O. Reischauer, *The Romanization of the Korean Language based upon its Phonetic Structure*, reprinted from THE TRANSACTIONS OF THE KOREA BRANCH OF THE ROYAL ASIATIC SOCIETY, Vol. XXIX (Seoul, 1939).

Official titles have been translated whenever possible, but in some cases they are given only in romanized form. Such translations as have been included are presented in order to give the reader an approximate idea of the functions of these officials and not as necessarily being in final or most correct form. In Appendix C may be found a brief outline of the Sui government in the latter part of the reign of Emperor Yang, that is after the changes of 607 mentioned in Chapter II.

The appendices and maps dealing with the geography of the Sui empire and the banditry and rebellions at the end of the dynasty need little explanation. The two principal lists of uprisings given in the dynastic annals have been translated, and an attempt has been made, by using reference works in Chinese, Japanese, and western languages, to locate on the maps and in the Index seventh century placenames included in the text and in these translations. It is hoped that in this way the reader will be aided to understand the unfamiliar geographical nomenclature and will be more easily able to follow the seemingly unrelated happenings in various parts of the country.

To the many professors and other friends who are in part responsible for whatever has been accomplished here, the writer offers his sincere appreciation, even though space does not permit a listing of their names.

He also wishes to express his thanks to the library staffs at Harvard University, Columbia University, the Library of Congress, and the University of California for generous assistance in the progress of this work.

To those who have read the manuscript of this book and helped in its evolution the writer is particularly indebted,— Professors Robert J. Kerner and Yoshi S. Kuno of the University of California, Dr. Arthur W. Hummel and Mr. Fêng Chia-shêng of the Library of Congress, and Professor William Hung of Yenching University. Especial gratitude is due Professor Peter A. Boodberg of the University of California for his patient, cheerful, and wise guidance during the early stages of bringing this material into acceptable form.

Many thanks are due to those scholars who have criticized this volume in the final stages of its preparation. The writer deeply appreciates the numerous constructive suggestions of Professor Homer H. Dubs of Duke University, Professor Charles Sidney Gardner of Harvard University, Dr. George A. Kennedy of Yale University, and Dr. Nancy Lee Swann of the Gest Oriental Library.

Finally, the writer is extremely grateful to Mr. Mortimer Graves and the other officers of the American Council of Learned Societies for their generous support in arranging for the publication of this study.

WOODBRIDGE BINGHAM

Berkeley, California
March 1, 1940

ABBREVIATIONS USED

BEFEO = *Bulletin de l'École Française d'Extrême-Orient*
CCBN = *Chung-kuo jên-ming ta-tz'ŭ-tien*: *Cyclopedia of Chinese Biographical Names*
CYCCC = Wên Ta-ya, *Ta T'ang ch'uang-yeh ch'i-chü-chu*
GBD = Giles, H. A., *A Chinese Biographical Dictionary*
HJAS = *Harvard Journal of Asiatic Studies*
TCTC = Ssŭ-ma Kuang, *Tzŭ-chih t'ung-chien*
TP = *T'oung Pao*

I. INTRODUCTION: EMPEROR YANG

THE MAN AND HIS TIMES

In 616 Emperor Yang,[1] a ruler who combined practical ability with imagination, one who the year before had entertained at his board the princes of neighboring states, a poet as well as a leader of able men, abandoned his capitals in the north of China and retired to the Yangtze valley never to return. Within two years he lay murdered, the Sui[2] dynasty was all but finished and the house of T'ang[3] began to extend its sway over the remnants of his empire. Wherein lay the causes for this rapid disintegration?

In most histories, whether in Chinese or western languages, the picture is simplified by failing to ascribe anything of greatness to Emperor Yang. Although he is well known for his love of fine literature and for his development of the Grand Canal, his achievements are considered as having been undertaken merely for his own personal enjoyment. Emperor Yang is depicted as one of the worst emperors China has ever known. He is characterized as a pleasure-loving madman chiefly interested in the

1. Yang-ti 煬帝, personal name Yang Kuang 楊廣, A.D. 569-618. Herbert A. Giles, *A Chinese Biographical Dictionary* [*GBD*] (London and Shanghai, 1898), No. 2393. *Chung-kuo jên-ming ta-tz'ŭ-tien: Cyclopedia of Chinese Biographical Names* [*CCBN*] (7th ed., Shanghai, 1930), p. 1214. Daily life and reign in *Sui-shu*, standard dynastic history by Wei Chêng, Ch'ang-sun Wu-chi, et al. (629-656. Photolithographic reprint of the Ch'ien-lung "palace edition" of 1739, published by T'ung-wên chü of Wu-chou, 1903), chs. 3 and 4; and in *Pei-shih*, standard history of the Northern Dynasties, 386-618, by Li Yen-shou, et al. (Completed ca. 664. Photo-lithographic reprint of the Ch'ien-lung "palace edition" of 1739, T'ung-wên shu-chü of Shanghai, 1894), ch. 12. In this study the abbreviation "ch." is used to indicate chapter or *chüan* according to whether the work referred to is in a western language or Chinese, respectively. Chinese characters for titles and authors of sources will be found in the Bibliography.
2. 隋, 581-618.
3. 唐, 618-906.

1

splendor of his palaces and the enjoyment of his women.[4] The fall of his house came naturally from the poor leadership of a ruler so corrupt.

Anyone' studying the records must admit that there is much to be said for this point of view. The Emperor was interested in enhancing the splendor of his court and of his empire. His ruthless ambition led him to the murder of his father and to the waste of imperial resources through such enterprises as his disastrous campaigns against the Koreans. In the subsequent pages there is presented abundant evidence of the weaknesses of Emperor Yang.

That these weaknesses seem to have been more important than his good points and that they contributed in large measure to the collapse of his empire must also be admitted. But from this fact has developed a distorted conception of the man. Little is available in western languages to indicate his real achievements or the fact that much of the greatness of the T'ang dynasty came directly from the foundations laid by the Sui emperors.

On the other hand the Chinese records give many evidences that Emperor Yang was an energetic, as well as an ambitious, ruler. There was much of serious purpose in his large-scale undertakings. Public works, literary endeavors, and foreign relations profited directly from his inspiration and guidance. He vigorously continued certain national policies of defence and expansion. These included further weakening of Turkish power and extension of Chinese authority to the oases of Turkistan. He himself personally visited the frontiers and led expeditions across the Liao River against Koguryŏ,[5] in northern Korea.

The purpose of the first part of this monograph then is to present impartially the facts concerning Emperor Yang and his reign as these facts emerge from the sources. A detailed survey

4. For two such characterizations of Emperor Yang see Léon Wieger, *Textes Historiques: Histoire politique de la Chine depuis l'origine, jusqu'en 1912* (2nd edition, Hsien-hsien, 1923), pp. 1275–1277, and 1295; and C. P. Fitzgerald, *Son of Heaven, A Biography of Li Shih-Min, founder of the T'ang Dynasty* (Cambridge, England, 1933), pp. 17–22.

5. See Chapter V.

of the Sui dynasty or even of the whole of Emperor Yang's reign is beyond the range of this study. The problem has been limited to research on the various phases of one reign and to determining so far as possible how much he personally was responsible and how much other factors were involved in the collapse of his empire.

Prior to the seventh century there was only one Chinese empire, the Han,[6] under which real unity had long endured. That dynasty ended in the third century of our era and gave way to one of those intervals of disunion which for longer or shorter periods have characterized the transition from one great dynasty to another. During this time China was first split up into what are known as the Three Kingdoms.[7] They were superseded by the Chin[8] which, though it lasted for a century and a half, was very weak and unified the whole country only for some thirty years at the end of the third century. The Chin was followed by a period of great confusion, known to the Chinese as the Nan-pei Ch'ao,[9] or the Southern and Northern Dynasties. Non-Chinese invaders set up various states in the north, while purely Chinese dynasties succeeded one another in the south. During this time no one house ruled the whole of China until the Sui dynasty reunited the country in 589.

The Sui followed the Northern (Pei) Chou[10] dynasty, which had controlled all the northern part of China since its conquest of the Northern (Pei) Ch'i[11] in 577. The founder of the Sui, Yang Chien, known to history as Emperor Wên (temple name

6. 漢, 206 B.C.—A.D. 220.
7. 三國, 221-265.
8. 晉, 265-420.
9. 南北朝, 420-589.
10. 北周, dynasty of the Yü-wên 宇文 family, 557-581. For Emperor Wên of the Sui dynasty's displacement of the Northern Chou dynasty, see *Sui-shu*, ch. 1, pp. 7a-13b. See also *Chou-shu* 周書 standard history of the Northern Chou, by Ling-hu Tê-fên 令狐德芬 [583-666; *GBD* 1264], et al., and *Pei-shih*, chs. 9, 10, etc. for the history of this dynasty.
11. 北齊, dynasty of the Kao 高 family, 550-577.

Kao-tsu),[12] superseded the Northern Chou in 581 and took as his own the capital Ch'ang-an.[13] Subsequently in 589 he brought China under unified rule with the conquest of Ch'ên,[14] the last of the Southern Dynasties.

Concerning this reunification of China through the conquest of the south by the north it is important to note that the northerners, although many bore old Chinese names, were of a mixed blood. The coming of great numbers of "barbarian" nomads into the north during the preceding centuries of invasion produced leaders who were not purely Chinese in the sense that the southerners were. A cleavage remained between the two. Although its influence cannot always be clearly distinguished, yet it must be

12. Kao-tsu Wên-ti 高祖文帝, personal name Yang Chien 楊堅, 541-604. *GBD* 2367. *CCBN*, p. 1213. Early life and reign in *Sui-shu*, chs. 1 and 2; *Pei-shih*, ch. 11.

13. Ch'ang-an 長安 is at present the official name of this ancient capital city in Shensi in northwestern China. However, it is more commonly known today as Sian 西安 (or Hsi-an-fu 西安府). In our texts it is also referred to as Ta-hsing-ch'êng 大興城, Ching-ch'êng 京城, or Ching-shih 京師. On the maps at the end of this volume the city is marked as Ching-chao-chün (京兆郡), since it was the center of the Sui commandery of that name. The commandery included two districts: Ta-hsing-hsien and Ch'ang-an-hsien.

Locations of seventh-century place names mentioned in the subsequent pages may be ascertained by reference to the Index and the maps.

14. 陳, 557-589. For the Sui conquest of Ch'ên, see *Sui-shu*, ch. 2, pp. 3a-4a; ch. 3, p. 1b; ch. 41, pp. 1a-6b; ch. 52; and other chs. (Ch. 41, pp. 1a-6b and ch. 52 are translated in August Pfizmaier, "Lebensbeschreibungen von Heerführern und Würdenträgern des Hauses Sui," *Denkschriften der kaiserlichen Akademie der Wissenschaften. Philosophisch-historische Classe*, Vol. XXXII [Vienna, 1882], pp. 369-377 and 341-345 respectively.) See also *Ch'ên-shu* 陳書, standard history of the Ch'ên dynasty, by Yao Ssŭ-lien 姚思廉 [d. 637] et al. (629-637). See especially chs. 6 and 31 (part of 6 and [all?] of 31 are translated in Pfizmaier, "Die letzten Zeiten des Reiches der Tsch'in," *Sitzungsberichte der kaiserlichen Akademie der Wissenschaften. Philosophischhistorische Classe*, Vol. XCVIII [Vienna, 1881], pp. 718-751). See also *Nan-shih* 南史, standard history of the Southern Dynasties, 420-589, by Li Yen-shou 李延壽, et al. (after 629).

kept in mind among the disruptive factors which are discussed in the following pages.

A significant example of this racial mixture is the marriage of ladies of the Tu-ku name into the noble Yang and Li families. Of the daughters of Tu-ku Hsin[15] one became an empress of the Sui dynasty, the Empress Wên-hsien[16] mentioned below, and another the mother of the first T'ang emperor.[17] The name Tu-ku is obviously not Chinese and was brought into China by northern "barbarians".

ACCESSION OF EMPEROR YANG

The Sui imperial court at Ch'ang-an in the beginning of the seventh century was permeated by intrigue. Although the empire had prospered during the last years of Emperor Wên, a succession of palace plots reached a climax at his death and the beginning of the reign of Emperor Yang.[17a]

The father, Yang Chien (Emperor Wên), had formerly, when he came to the throne, proclaimed Yang Yung,[18] his eldest son

15. 獨孤信, 503–557. *CCBN*, p. 1587. Biography in *Chou-shu*, ch. 16, and *Pei-shih*, ch. 61.

16. 文獻皇后 of the Tu-ku 獨孤 family, 544–602. *CCBN*, p. 1587. Biography in *Sui-shu*, ch. 36 (Tr. Pfizmaier, "Darlegungen aus der Geschichte des Hauses Sui," *Sitzungsber., d. k. Ak. d. Wiss. Phil.-hist. Classe*, Vol. XCVII [Vienna, 1881], pp. 649 653) and in *Pei-shih*, ch. 14.

17. See the Genealogical Table, Appendix B, for an outline of these relationships.

17a. While this study is in the press further significant details concerning the Emperors Wên and Yang, and which constitute a valuable supplement to this chapter, have appeared under the heading "The Rise and Fall of the House of Yang" in the second article by Peter A. Boodberg, entitled "Marginalia to the Histories of the Northern Dynasties," *Harvard Journal of Asiatic Studies [HJAS]*, Vol. IV, Nos. 3 and 4 (December, 1939), pp. 253–270. Note also his complete genealogical table of "The Family of Yang Chung," *ibid.*, pp. 282–283.

18. 楊勇, (d. 604). *CCBN*, p. 1268. Biography in *Sui-shu*, ch. 45 (Tr. Pfizmaier, "Darlegungen . . . des Hauses Sui," pp. 627–649) and in *Pei-shih*, ch. 71. Here and elsewhere biographical dates in parenthesis are those for which no precise references have been found.

and family heir, to be imperial Heir Apparent.[19]   The latter had long enjoyed the confidence of his father, but through the plotting of the Empress Wên-hsien and of Yang Kuang (later Emperor Yang), Yung was degraded and made a commoner while Yang Kuang became Heir Apparent.[20]

Yang Kuang took every advantage to gain precedence and came into the good graces of the Emperor by catering to his father's attitude in regard to personal favorites.   The annals of Emperor Yang say:

> At the beginning of his career Yang Kuang,[21] realizing that he was a "guardian prince,"[22] and in order of succession had no right to the throne, always camouflaged his real feelings and glossed over his actions in order to angle for empty fame.   He secretly entertained schemes for seizing the succession.
>
> At this time, Emperor Wên put his full trust in the Empress Wên-hsien, while by nature he shunned secondary consorts.   The Heir Apparent Yung [privately] had many favorites in his palace, and so he lost the love of his parents.
>
> As to Yang Kuang, whenever he begot sons in the ladies' quarters, he raised none of them,[23] thus showing that he indulged in no extramarital relations and winning the affection of the Empress [his mother].[24]

The parents believed in monogamy.[25]   Their son Yung did

19. K'ai-huang 開皇, 1st year, 2nd moon, day 3 (March 6, 581). *Sui-shu*, ch. 1, p. 14a.

20. K'ai-huang 20th year, 10th moon, day 2, and 11th moon, day 25 (November 20 and December 13, 600).   *Sui-shu*, ch. 2, pp. 14b–15a; ch. 3, p. 2a, and ch. 36, p. 5b.   See also ch. 45.

21. This passage is from the annals of Emperor Yang and hence refers to him throughout as "the Emperor".   His personal name is used here in order to avoid confusion.

22. *Fan wang* 藩王.   In this position it was his duty to fight in behalf of the dynasty and empire although he was definitely not in line to succeed his father.

23. *Chieh pu yü-chih* 皆不育之.

24. *Sui-shu*, ch. 4, p. 15a.   The last statement may refer to Emperor Yang's wife, but probably does not.

25. Cf. Peter A. Boodberg, "Marginalia to the Histories of the Northern Dynasties," *Harvard Journal of Asiatic Studies*, Vol. III, Nos. 3 and 4 (December, 1938), p. 232.

not conform to this belief and hence lost his place in their affections, while Kuang seems to have let his offspring die in order to give the impression that he was not interested in concubines. By a friendly and liberal attitude, Yang Kuang also received praise from officials and servants.[26] Thus he gained position and power at the expense of his brother.

Later, when Emperor Wên lay ill and received accusations of improper conduct against Kuang from the Lady Ch'ên,[27] the Emperor's favorite consort, he summoned Yang Yung with what appears to have been the desire to restore him as Heir Apparent. Yang Kuang is alleged to have ended all possibility of counterplots by having Emperor Wên murdered and taking the Lady Ch'ên for his own.[28] Two brief quotations from the *Sui History* indicate the sequence of events as recorded by the T'ang scholars.

At first when Emperor Wên was ill in bed in the Jên-shou Palace,[29] the *Fu-jên*[30] [i.e. the Lady Ch'en] was attending on his illness together with the Imperial Heir Apparent Yang Kuang. When at dawn she went out to change her clothes she was improperly accosted by the Heir Apparent. The *Fu-jên* resisted him and succeeded in escaping.

When she returned to where the Emperor was, the Emperor, being amazed that her facial appearance was unusual, asked the reason. The *Fu-jên* in tears said: "The Heir Apparent has shown himself devoid of any sense of propriety." The Emperor angered said: "The brute! How is he worthy to succeed to the Great Undertaking [i.e., the rule of the empire]? Tu-ku has indeed put me in error." By Tu-ku he meant the Empress Hsien.

26. *Sui-shu*, ch. 4, pp. 15a–15b.
27. 陳氏, 577–605. *CCBN*, p. 648. Biography in *Sui-shu*, ch. 36 and in *Pei-shih*, ch. 14. The phrase "Lady Ch'ên" is intended as an abbreviation of the more literal "Lady of Clan Ch'ên," meaning that she originally came from this family. It is not a title like *Fu-jên* 夫人, a phrase which might perhaps be translated "Lady" but which is untranslated here in order to avoid confusion.
28. Emperor Wên's death occurred in Jên-shou 仁壽 4th year, 7th moon, day 44 (August 13, 604); *Sui-shu*, ch. 2, p. 21a. See also ch. 3, p. 2a, and ch. 36, pp. 6a–7a.
29. Jên-shou kung 仁壽宮.
30. See n. 26.

Therefore he called the President of the Board of War[31] Liu Shu[32] and the Vice President of the Department of the Imperial Chancellery[33] Yüan Yen[34] and said: "Summon my son." Liu Shu and the other were about to call the Heir Apparent when the Emperor said: "[I mean] Yung." Liu Shu and Yüan Yen went out of the side-hall to draw up the imperial message.[35] When finished they showed it to the Left Vice President of the Department of State Affairs[36] Yang Su.[37] Yang Su told this matter to the Heir Apparent.

The Heir Apparent sent Chang Hêng[38] into the sleeping palace. Following that he commanded the *Fu-jên* and those of the ladies' quarters who were attending on [Emperor Wên in his] illness all to go out and proceed to another room. Shortly after it was heard that the Emperor had died.[39]

This is the most detailed account we have concerning Emperor Wên's death. It is found in the biography of the Lady Ch'ên and not in the imperial dynastic annals, where a natural death is indicated. Hence it may be considered either less authentic than the version of the annals or merely relegated to a woman's biography in order not to bring the story of such a heinous crime into the biography of an emperor. It should be noted, however, that this account is repeated in Ssŭ-ma Kuang's famous history, the *Comprehensive Mirror for Aid in Government*.[40]

31. *Ping-pu shang-shu* 兵部尙書.
32. 柳述. *CCBN*, p. 660. Biography in *Sui-shu*, ch. 47, and in *Pei-shih*, ch. 64.
33. *Huang-mên shih-lang* 黃門侍郎.
34. 元巖, d. 617. *CCBN*, p. 33. Biography in *Sui-shu*, ch. 62, and *Pei-shih*, ch. 75.
35. *Ch'ih-shu* 勅書.
36. *Tso p'u-yeh* 左僕射.
37. 楊素, d. 606. *GBD*, 2408. *CCBN*, p. 1272. Biography in *Sui-shu*, ch. 48 (Tr. Pfizmaier, "Darlegungen ... des Hauses Sui," pp. 658-685) and in *Pei-shih*, ch. 41.
38. 張衡, d. 612. *CCBN*, p. 971. Biography in *Sui-shu*, ch. 56, and in *Pei-shih*, ch. 74.
39. *Sui-shu*, ch. 36, pp. 6a-6b.
40. *Tzŭ-chih t'ung-chien* [*TCTC*] by Ssŭ-ma Kuang (1086. Photolithographic reprint of the 1132 reprint, Vols. XCIX–CLXXVIII in *Ssŭ-pu ts'ung-k'an*, Shanghai, 1922), ch. 180, pp. 2a–2b.

In Emperor Yang's biography the following general remarks are given concerning his conduct at that time:

From the time when Emperor Wên was at death's door during his critical illness and up to the time of the period of mourning his son's incestuous dissipation was unrestrained. . . .[41]

Such conduct before and at the beginning of his reign, if it actually took place, may have profoundly influenced subsequent events. But only by an objective analysis of these events can we begin to see the history in its true perspective.

In this study we are chiefly concerned with Emperor Yang's career as a ruler and the causes which led to his downfall. For data concerning either his earlier life or his reign, we have to rely on the official historians of the early T'ang period, men who had turned against the Sui dynasty. Their work, the *Sui History* (*Sui-shu*), is the most reliable record available of the events of this time. But, with their natural bias in favor of the T'ang dynasty and the great emphasis given to personal factors, they appear in their summaries to place too great stress upon the faults of Emperor Yang and show no sympathy with what in many cases may have been worthy intentions.[42]

Emperor Yang, for example, is described as an extravagant emperor, deceitful, suspicious, and too much given to the pleasures of the palace. He is said to have been vindictive towards any officials who did not agree with his views. His foreign undertakings were too expensive and he extended foreign trade simply to gratify personal tastes. Under his rule, officialdom became demoralized through bribery and unjust punishment.[43] In

41. *Sui-shu*, ch. 4, p. 15b.
42. A modern Chinese writer explains the bias of the official writers concerning Emperor Yang in the following words: "The moral approach of the Chinese historians prevented them from understanding the political meaning of Yang Ti's achievements as well as his crimes." Ch'ao-ting Chi, *Key Economic Areas in Chinese History as Revealed in the Development of Public Works for Water-Control* (London, 1936), p. 121.
43. *Sui-shu*, ch. 4, pp. 15b–16a. See also pp. 16b–18a. References to the Sui annals, beginning with Ta-yeh 大業 9th year (613) and

conformity with the Confucian theory of personal imperial responsibility, the historians seem to have made much of every weakness of the Sui emperors and of any line of conduct disapproved by the scholars to show that the ruin of the dynasty and the disorder at its end naturally followed from these factors. Not only is Emperor Yang represented as an emperor under whose reign disaster would be inevitable, but the personal responsibility is transferred back to his father for having unwisely changed the succession. May not such conclusions be subject to re-evaluation? A thorough understanding of Emperor Yang and the decline of the dynasty can be reached only by a careful study of all parts of the *Sui History*.

Preliminary research in that direction has been attempted. Statements of fact have been used in preference to the opinions of historians, but it has not yet been possible to determine entirely what passages are most reliable. For example, the section dealing with the reign of Emperor Yang in the "Monograph on Food and Commodities" of the *Sui History* is uniformly unfavorable towards that emperor and hence must be used with caution. Much material from this chapter has been included, however, as it contains information not found elsewhere.

With this in mind, let us turn to the annals and biographies, as well as monographs, to note briefly the main factors in the situation. First of all, what were the internal conditions and what were some of the projects undertaken within the state?

including the passage here referred to, have all been checked in *Pei-shih*, ch. 12.

II. CONSTRUCTION OF PUBLIC WORKS, 605-608

INTERNAL ADMINISTRATION

When he ascended the throne Emperor Yang succeeded to the control of a prosperous empire.[1] His father had been a careful and economical ruler. The son took advantage of peace and plenty to increase the activities of the state as well as to expand it beyond its former limits. This development is seen in a revision of the administrative system and of state education, the maintaining of imperial establishments at three capitals, an extensive program of public works, and the promotion of territorial expansion.

The state of Sui times was a centralized bureaucracy based for its support on the Confucian scholars. The administrative system was much the same as that of the preceding and following dynasties.[2] Some reorganization was undertaken under Emperor Yang. The alterations were largely a matter of "rectification of names", an idea which goes back to the time of Confucius, and the abolition of some titles. This was carried out according to a plan drawn up by the Emperor's minister, P'ei Chü,[3] in 607.[4]

1. *Sui-shu*, ch. 24, p. 17a.
2. See Appendix C for an outline of the Sui system.
3. 裴矩, ca. 548-627. *GBD* 1628. *CCBN*, p. 1382. Biography in *Sui-shu*, ch. 67; *Pei-shih*, ch. 38; *T'ang-shu*, standard dynastic history by Ou-yang Hsiu, Sung Ch'i, et al. (1060. Photolithographic reprint of the Ch'ien-lung "palace edition" of 1739, T'ung-wên shu-chü of Shanghai, 1884), ch. 100; and *Chiu T'ang-shu*, standard dynastic history by Liu Hsü, et al. (945. Photo-lithographic reprint of the Ch'ien-lung "palace edition" of 1739, T'ung-wên shu-chü of Shanghai, 1884), ch. 63. The first three of these *chüan* are translated in Fritz Jäger, "Leben und Werk des P'ei Kü. Ein Kapitel aus der chinesischen Kolonialgeschichte," *Ostasiatische Zeitschrift*, Vol. IX (Berlin, 1920-22), pp. 81-115, 216-231.
4. *Sui-shu*, ch. 3, p. 8b; ch. 67, p. 10b. See also *ibid.*, ch. 28, pp. 22b-33a, for the governmental changes of 607; synopsis in *TCTC*, ch. 180, p. 17a. Cf. Jäger, "P'ei Kü", p. 95, n. 8.

11

Changes were made in the names of the departments and bureaus of the central government, as well as of some military commands. In the local administration "prefectures" (*chou*) were abolished, and "commanderies" (*chün*) became the chief units of administration.[5] In addition, alterations were made in the size and number of commanderies and "districts" (*hsien*).[6]

The connection between administration and education became particularly important in this time of reunification and strengthening of the centralized state. The two great state examinations for the doctorate which were of most importance in T'ang times, the *chin-shih* and the *ming-ching*,[7] originated under the Sui dynasty. The *chin-shih* was created during the reign of Emperor Yang and continued to be a mark of high scholarship and official eligibility until the end of the Manchu period.[8] Emperor Yang's promotion of state education dates from the beginning of his reign,[9] and at this time also much interest was shown in the collection and creation of literature, both by the Emperor himself and by the scholars whom he gathered at his court.[10]

These efforts of the Sui rulers, and Emperor Yang in particular, may be considered an integral part of the great administrative and cultural development of T'ang times. They were elements of strength, and it was not in these lines that the Sui organization failed, nor brought about results fatal to the continuance of the dynasty. In the matter of public works, however, we find a

5. *Chou* 州 and *chün* 郡. *Sui-shu*, ch. 3, p. 8b; ch. 28, pp. 22b–23a and 32a.

6. *Hsien* 縣. Henri Maspero, "Le Protectorat Général d'Annam sous les T'ang. Essai de Géographie Historique," *BEFEO*, Vol. X (1910), p. 565.

7. 進士 and 明經.

8. Robert Des Rotours, *Le Traité des Examens traduit de la Nouvelle Histoire des T'ang (Chap. XLIV, XLV)*, Bibliothèque de l'Institut des Hautes Études Chinoises, Vol. II (Paris, 1932), pp. 27–28 and p. 127, n. 2.

9. See the edict of Ta-yeh 1st year, intercalary 7th moon, day 13 (September 6, 605), in *Sui-shu*, ch. 3, pp. 5b–6b. Cf. John Knight Shryock, *The Origin and Development of the State Cult of Confucius: an Introductory Study* (New York, 1932), pp. 121–122.

10. *Sui-shu*, ch. 32 (first part of the "Monograph on Literature").

program pushed too far, further than the newly unified empire was able to support.

The economic development of China preceding the Sui period and during that time is recorded in the "Monograph on Food and Commodities" in the *Sui History*.[11] Definitive research on Emperor Yang's reign awaits a critical translation of this entire essay. Meanwhile, many of the most significant reasons for the decline of the Sui may be understood from a study of the more important politico-economic factors of the period and in particular the stupendous public works undertaken during the administration of the last Sui emperor.

NEW CAPITAL AT LO-YANG

At the start of his reign Emperor Yang was able to effect a temporary reduction in the drafts of forced labor required by the state,[12] but his plans for a splendid imperial establishment, together with a necessity for consolidating the economic basis of the state, led him soon to return to the other extreme of labor conscription on a large scale. One of the first projects which he undertook was the founding of a new capital, an "eastern capital", Tung-tu, at Lo-yang.[13] The capital of his father, Ch'ang-an, was still the center of government, but was now termed the "western capital", or Hsi-tu.[14] At Lo-yang he built palaces and gardens filled with rare plants and animals. The magnitude of the

11. This chapter, *Sui-shu*, ch. 24 (*Shih-huo chih* 食貨志), has been translated in an unpublished manuscript by Miss Rhea C. Blue of the University of California.

12. "... The emperor abolished the drafting [for public service] of wives, and of female and male slaves. Even men were not considered able-bodied [liable to draft] until the age of twenty-two." *Sui-shu*, ch. 24, p. 17a. "Twenty-two" here would mean twenty-one according to our reckoning.

13. 東都, 洛陽. Ancient city in Honan province. The Chou name Lo-i 洛邑 is found in some of the T'ang writings. On the maps at the end of this volume the city is marked as Ho-nan-chün (河南郡), since it was the center of a commandery. The commandery included two districts: Ho-nan-hsien and Lo-yang-hsien.

14. 西都.

work can be appreciated from the huge numbers of people involved.

> Every moon the Emperor conscripted two million laborers. In order to fill the new capital he moved in the people from the suburban areas of Lo-chou[15] [i.e. the prefecture of Lo-yang] and several ten thousand families of rich merchants and great traders from all the prefectures of the empire.[16]

He ordered large timber from the region south of the Yangtze to be brought to this new capital, a matter involving much labor and hardship for those doing the work. The localities on the way were required to undertake the transport by a relay system.

> Unbroken processions [i.e. of these transport corps] extended one after another for a thousand *li*. Among the laborers drafted for the eastern capital four or five out of every ten fell prostrate and died on account of being under such great pressure. Every moon in carrying the dead bodies east to Ch'êng-kao and north to Ho-yang[17] the carts were always within view of each other on the road.[18]

GRAIN STORAGE AND THE GRAND CANAL

The Emperor also planned a capital in the Yangtze valley at Chiang-tu (modern Yang-chou[19]), and arranged to travel between north and south in comfort and magnificence. This is one reason for the development of the Grand Canal and was a factor in the lavishness and expense of the undertaking. The other and main reason was the necessity for provisioning the capitals further north.

The Sui state depended very largely upon the land tax, payments for which were made in the form of grain tribute from the

15. 洛州.
16. *Sui-shu*, ch. 24, p. 17a. Cf. *ibid.*, ch. 3, pp. 5a–5b. "In Ta-yeh 2nd year, 1st moon, day 58 [February 18, 606], Tung-tu was completed . . . " *Sui-shu*, ch. 3, p. 6b.
17. Ch'êng-kao: 城皋 (or 成皋), northwest of present Ssǔ-shui 汜水. Name changed to Ssǔ-shui in 598; *Sui-shu*, ch. 30, p. 2a. Ho-yang: 河陽. Both places are on the Yellow River northeast of Lo-yang.
18. *Sui-shu*, ch. 24, pp. 17a and 17b.
19. 揚州. At present this town is again called Chiang-tu 江都.

various parts of the empire. The political focus of this empire was in the north, the traditional center of power and the strategic base for defense of the vulnerable steppe frontier. On the other hand, the key economic area was not, as it had been earlier, in the valleys of the Wei and Yellow Rivers, but was now shifting to the valley of the Yangtze. In this highly productive region surplus quantities of tribute rice could be raised and sent north to provision the central government. Hence it was of vital importance for the Sui rulers to develop and maintain a transport system linking the north and south.[20]

Emperor Wên had employed a system of four state granaries to keep Ch'ang-an supplied in times of flood and drought. These granaries were established in 583 for specific purposes in four different districts in the Yellow River valley. Thus grain from modern Shansi and the north China plain could be stored and trans-shipped to Ch'ang-an. Of the four granaries one, the Li-yang Granary,[21] was in Honan about ten miles southwest of present Chün-hsien[22] along the route to the northeast. Two were between Lo-yang and Ch'ang-an. The Ch'ang-p'ing Granary[23] was in the vicinity of modern Shan-hsien,[24] east of T'ung-kuan.[25] The other, the Kuang-t'ung Granary,[26] was west of T'ung-kuan at the mouth of the Wei River.[27] The fourth, or Ho-yang Granary,[28] was near Lo-yang.[29]

20. Cf. Ch'ao-ting Chi, *Key Economic Areas in Chinese History as Revealed in the Development of Public Works for Water-Control* (London, 1936), *passim*.
21. Li-yang ts'ang 黎陽倉.
22. 濬縣.
23. Ch'ang-p'ing ts'ang 常平倉.
24. 陝縣.
25. 潼關.
26. Kuang-t'ung ts'ang 廣通倉. Presumably this is the one later known as Yung-fêng ts'ang 永豐倉. The name Kuang was Emperor Yang's personal name and hence taboo during his reign.
27. Wei-ho 渭河.
28. Ho-yang ts'ang 河陽倉.
29. *Sui-shu*, ch. 24, p. 14a.

To facilitate the transport of grain tribute between these granaries Emperor Wên in 584 opened a canal along the line of an old Han water route. This connected Ch'ang-an with T'ung-kuan and enabled boats to avoid the uncertain risks of navigation on the Wei River. Thus the communications between the Yellow River valley and the Sui capital in the west were provided for some years prior to the conquest of south China in 589.[30]

By the time of Emperor Yang the need was felt for more granaries in the vicinity of Lo-yang and a further development of communications with the south. The Emperor extended the storage system begun under his father's direction by establishing two additional granaries. These were the Hsing-lo Granary and Hui-lo Granary, to the northeast of Lo-yang.[31]

At the same time work was commenced on the "Grand Canal". This term refers to a series of water-courses joining North China with the Yangtze Valley and includes the Wei valley canal mentioned above. It is to be differentiated from the modern Grand Canal system which follows a somewhat different route.[32]

Old canals and streams were extended and united into one main waterway. This may be considered the outstanding achievement among the public works of Emperor Yang's reign. Brief statements in the *Sui History* show how the development of a magnificent imperial highway was combined with construction for the sake of economic communications.

The most important section of the canal system was between the newly created eastern capital and the Yangtze.[33] Work on

30. *Sui-shu*, ch. 1, p. 21b, and ch. 24, pp. 14a–15a. Dr. Chi has translated the edict directing the construction of this canal but he makes it appear that the construction took place about twenty years later under the direction of Emperor Yang. Chi, *Key Economic Areas*, pp 119–120.

31. 興洛倉 and 廻洛倉; *Sui-shu*, ch. 24, p. 17a.

32. See Map II. Cf. Albert Herrmann, *Historical and Commercial Atlas oj China*, Harvard-Yenching Institute Monograph Series, Vol. I (Cambridge, 1935), p. 36.

33. The course of this section of the canal has been entered on Maps I and II in accordance with the conclusions of Aoyama Sadao in his "Study on the Canal *Pien* (汴河) in the Period *T'ang* and *Sung*,"

this part was undertaken in 605, the first year of Emperor Yang's reign.

... From Pan-chu[34] he led the Yellow River to flow into the Huai River[35] and to the sea, calling this the "Imperial Stream."[36] On the banks of the stream he built an "Imperial Road", and planted it with willows.[37]

For the labor on this route and its connection with his palace at Lo-yang, the government is said to have employed on a single day over a million men and women workers.[38]

This canal was indeed an imperial highway. From Lo-yang to Chiang-tu the Emperor moved in magnificent state. He ordered the construction of a variety of splendid barges, "dragon boats" and others, for himself and his suite. Specially recruited labor, palace servants dressed in brocade, pulled the boats by means of green ropes. When the Emperor travelled with his retinue, the fleet was over two hundred *li* in length.[39]

Rigorous measures were taken to insure adequate supplies for these elaborate trips.

All the prefectures and districts through which they passed were ordered to supply meals and to offer provisions. Those officials who provided abundantly were given additional rank while those who were deficient were punished even unto death.[40]

In this manner a through waterway was inaugurated between the Yangtze and the Yellow River valley. A few years later other long extensions were added both in the north and south. These will be mentioned further on as they fit into the later

---

Tôhô Gakuhô, Tokyo, No. 2 (December, 1931), pp. 1–49 (especially Chap. II, Sec. 3, "The position of the Canal Pien in the Sui period").
34. 板渚, on the Yellow River east of the mouth of the Lo.
35. Huai-shui 淮水, in northern Anhui.
36. Yü-ho 御河, also known as T'ung-chi-ch'ü 通濟渠.
37. *Sui-shu*, ch. 24, p. 17a.
38. Ta-yeh 1st year, 3rd moon, day 48 (April 14, 605). *Sui-shu*, ch. 3, p. 5b.
39. *Sui-shu*, ch. 24, p. 17b.
40. *Sui-shu*, ch. 24, p. 17b.

events of Emperor Yang's reign. All these waterways were constructed under harsh conditions of forced labor which have been the subject of comment by historians ever since.

The oppression of the people involved in this canal-building and in other similar projects is not to be attributed simply to grand schemes initiated by the Emperor for his own political power and the gratification of his vanity. The whole ruling class of Confucian officials depended for their support upon the central government and the accumulation of surplus resources. Dr. Ch'ao-ting Chi has given an apt summary of this situation in his illuminating book, *Key Economic Areas in Chinese History as Revealed in the Development of Public Works for Water-Control*:

"... the Chinese state was frankly based upon the theory of class rule, and class rule meant the concentration of surplus resources, very often including a large proportion of the necessities of life squeezed from the people, as an instrument of power and to satisfy the extravagant demands of the ruling group. The concentration of resources demanded canal building and canal building in turn demanded a further concentration of resources, which invariably lead to excessive taxation and a cruel and large-scale programme of forced labour."[41]

Harsh exactions of wealth and labor are to be found also in the search for rare objects used for decoration of imperial equipment and still more in the work on the Great Wall. In all these cases the principal source of information is that same "Monograph on Food and Commodities"[42] which is so hostile to Emperor Yang. Hence the figures may have been exaggerated and the picture painted darker than it actually was. But in any case the conditions must have been those of real hardship for the people who bore the burdens of his government.

IMPERIAL EQUIPMENT

Rare objects used to enhance the splendor of the imperial court were brought in through special requisitions. The lavish

41. Pp. 121–122.
42. *Sui-shu*, ch. 24.

equipment of Emperor Yang's chariots, banners and other decorative contrivances taxed the whole empire.

... In general all bone, horn, ivory, hides, hair and feathers which could be used for decorating utensils or which were suitable for making hair and feather decorations and pennants [?] were exacted. The requisitions were so urgent that what was ordered in the morning had to be provided by evening.

The people sought and caught with net and snare all through the open country [until] on water and land birds and beasts were almost exterminated. And yet the people were not able to contribute [all the things required], and hence were forced to buy from the influential and rich families who had them stored up. Prices [of these objects] rose sharply . . .[43]

These requisitions occurred in 606 when the new eastern capital was completed and Emperor Yang made his official entry. The severity of the exactions occasioned by this event was lessened through a year's grace in the collection of revenue.[44] Thus some relief was afforded the tax-payers.

GREAT WALL

Other large scale undertakings were carried on simultaneously or planned for the near future. Emperor Yang continued the work of his predecessors, including his father, in fortifying his borders along the line of the Great Wall. This policy is important not only for foreign affairs, but also as one of the huge public works constructed during the early years of the reign.

In two successive years, 607 and 608, the Emperor went north to the borders of modern Shansi and on each occasion ordered large numbers of men to work on the Great Wall. The working period, which came during the summer, seems to have been of short duration. This probably was arranged in order not to keep the peasants too long away from their farms, also because of the difficulty in provisioning a large force of labor, and what may have been the disastrous results of the first effort. In any case the

43. *Sui-shu*, ch. 24, pp. 17b and 18a.
44. *Sui-shu*, ch. 3, p. 7a.

recorded figures are very large and are evidently intended as additional evidence of the severity of Emperor Yang's rule.

In one day[45] during 607 more than a million men were sent out to work on the border fortifications extending across the north of present Shansi from Yü-lin in the west to the Tzŭ River in the east.[46] The cost in human life was tremendous: five or six out of every ten died. After ten days, the work was stopped.[47] The next year the Emperor inspected the work himself[48] and again sent over two hundred thousand to continue the construction from Yü-lin.[49]

Enough has been written to indicate the harshness of the Sui system of forced labor as a background for the rebellious movements of Emperor Yang's last years. Large scale public works were continued and the internal situation was further complicated by flood, drought, and conscription for military purposes. These changes in the economic conditions after 608 will be mentioned chronologically in relation to other important events of the time.

In all these internal projects undertaken during the reign of Emperor Yang we may see an element of greatness and an element of weakness for the state. The expansion of imperial power and the magnitude of the public works completed at this time reflect the grandiose character of the Emperor's own imagination and enterprise. And yet such an undertaking as the strengthening of the Great Wall fortification system involved so much expense and suffering for the people that one may be inclined to overlook the larger policy of which it was a part. The defense of the northern border against the Eastern Turks was of utmost importance for the Chinese state during the early seventh century.[50]

Relations with these neighbors to the North was only one

45. Ta-yeh 3rd year, 7th moon, day 13 (August 27, 607).
46. Yü-lin 楡林; Tzŭ-ho 紫河.
47. Sui-shu, ch. 3, p. 11a.
48. Ta-yeh 4th year, 3rd moon, day 2 (April 12, 608). Sui-shu, ch. 3, p. 12a. See also ibid., ch. 24, p. 18a.
49. 7th moon, day 18 (August 26). Sui-shu, ch. 3, p. 12b.
50. See Chapter IV for Emperor Yang's relations with the Eastern Turks.

among the varied connections involving the Sui state with peoples beyond the borders of China. Most notable for the early years of Emperor Yang's reign was a successful policy of territorial expansion. This attempt to enlarge the Sui boundaries is important from the beginning to the end of the reign. And yet grand schemes led only to temporary glory. Even more than construction of public works, relations with neighboring peoples tended towards disintegration of the empire.

III. FOREIGN RELATIONS

SOUTH AND EAST

In the early years of Emperor Yang's rule foreign relations were satisfactory for China. Imperial prestige was enhanced. Trade connections became more profitable, and the revenues of the state were increased. These were some of the more important motives and definite results in the pushing out of Sui boundaries to include more territory.

In this Chinese expansion Sui relations with neighboring states follow in some measure directly from the Emperor's internal policy. Thus in the *Sui History* chapter on "Food and Commodities" just after the description of the search for rarities and the sharp rise in the prices of such things as fine feathers, we find the statement:

Accordingly the Emperor employed the Secretary for Military Colonies Ch'ang Chün[1] [who] went as an envoy to the state of Ch'ih-t'u[2] and reached Lo-ch'a[3] [during the journey].[4]

His voyage to the south occupied the years 608 to 610.[5]

1. *T'un-t'ien chu-shih* Ch'ang Chün 屯田主事常駿. For his journey to the state of Ch'ih-t'u see *Sui-shu*, ch. 82, pp. 4b–5b.
2. 赤土國, present Songkla (Singora) in lower Siam, or Sumatra. For its history in these times see *Sui-shu*, ch. 82 (Tr. Pfizmaier, "Die fremdländischen Reiche zu den Zeiten der Sui," *Sitzungsber. d. k. Ak. d. Wiss. Phil.-hist. Classe*, Vol. XCVII [Vienna, 1881], pp. 433–439) and *Pei-shih*, ch. 95.
3. 羅刹 (*Sui-shu*, ch. 3, p. 12a, gives Lo-chi 羅剎), a country probably in the East Indies. For a brief account of the state of Lo-ch'a see *T'ung-tien* by Tu Yu (801. Wu-ying-tien edition, Canton, 1871), ch. 188, pp. 22b–23a. It has been suggested that the words 致羅刹 (or 羅剎) may mean "to get 'fine woven fabrics' " and does not refer to a country, but the *T'ung-tien* definitely refers to Lo-ch'a as a state and makes such a meaning very unlikely.
4. *Sui-shu*, ch. 24, p. 18a.
5. *Sui-shu*, ch. 3, p. 12a, and ch. 82, pp. 4b–5b. *TCTC*, ch. 18, p. 2a,

This mission of Ch'ang Chün had been preceded by military and diplomatic expansion to the south and east. Early in 603 the general Liu Fang[6] was sent to suppress a rebellion in Chiao-chou[7] (present Tonkin), long a part of the Chinese empire. From there he went on in 605 to take the capital of Champa, Lin-i[8] or Indrapura, south of the present Tourane on the coast of Indo-China, and to effect a temporary Chinese suzerainty in that region.[9]

Envoys from Japan (Wo-kuo)[10] had come to the Sui court in 600 and 607. These missions came from the Japanese government in the time of the great Regent Shōtoku Taishi, the man who was largely responsible for starting his country in the direction of a strong centralized state on the Chinese pattern. He aimed to place Japan on as firm a basis as the Sui empire. This ideal is shown in the letter carried by the envoy of 607. It was worded in such a way as to claim equality with China. The opening words were, "The Son of Heaven of the Sunrise Land

---

agrees with the Sui annals (ch. 3) in placing the start of the journey in Ta-yeh 4th year (608). *Sui-shu*, ch. 82, p. 4b, reads Ta-yeh 3rd year (607).

6. 劉方. *CCBN*, pp. 1435-1436. Biography in *Sui-shu*, ch. 53, and in *Pei-shih*, ch. 73.

7. 交州, also known in Sui times as Chiao-chih-chün 交趾 (or 阯) 郡. See *Sui-shu*, ch. 31, p. 12b. Liu Fang was despatched in Jên-shou 2nd year, 12th moon (January 18–February 15, 603); *Sui-shu*, ch. 2, p. 17b.

8. 林邑. For the history of Lin-i in these times see *Sui-shu*, ch. 82 (Tr. Pfizmaier, "Fremdländischen Reiche," pp. 429–439) and *Pei-shih*, ch. 95.

9. *Sui-shu*, ch. 3, p. 5b.

10. 倭國. (In *Sui-shu*, ch. 81, the name 俀國 [T'ui-kuo] is used. Other *chüan* in the *Sui-shu* and other dynastic histories, before and afterwards, as far as I know, always use the name Wo-kuo.) For an account of Japan in these times and of this interchange of missions see *Sui-shu*, ch. 81 (Tr. Pfizmaier, *op. cit.*, pp. 422–429); *Pei-shih*, ch. 94; Yoshi S. Kuno, *Japanese Expansion on the Asiatic Continent*, Vol. I (Berkeley, 1937), pp. 15–16, and 229–231; Robert Karl Reischauer, *Early Japanese History* (*c. 40 B.C.–A.D. 1167*) (Princeton, 1937), Part A, pp. 48, 49, 141.

writes the Son of Heaven of the Sunset Land."[11]   Emperor Yang
was displeased at what he considered Japanese presumption.
Nevertheless, he sent an envoy to Japan in the following year.
Japanese missions came again to China in 608 and 610.[12]
From this time on for many centuries the Japanese came to
Sui and T'ang China.   Their country was deeply influenced by
Confucian and Buddhist ideas.   The connection between the
two countries is of vital importance for the study of Japan but is
of much less significance for the history of Sui China.

In the early years of his reign, Emperor Yang three times
undertook offensive operations against the state of Liu-ch'iu[13]
on the present island of Formosa.   On the last occasion a large
army was sent.   Many prisoners of war were captured.[14]   No
regular relations, however, were established between China and
Liu-ch'iu.

In these areas to the east and south, Liu-ch'iu, Japan, and the
states of Indo-China, Sui interests in the time of Emperor Yang
extended far beyond the borders of China.   But these interests
were relatively unimportant and had very little connection with
the larger policies of the state as compared with Sui contacts along
the northern borders.

WESTERN REGIONS

From the trans-Asiatic trade routes in the northwest to Korea
in the east, any event along the northern frontier might have
important consequences for China.   Emperor Yang realized this
fact and spent vast sums in attempting to control the neighboring
regions.   Loss of prestige on that frontier, together with internal
weakness, were directly responsible for the collapse of his dynasty.
The Emperor's ambition and cupidity, plus the natural exten-

11. *Sui-shu*, ch. 81, pp. 15b–16a.   Translation from Reischauer, *op.
cit.*, p. 141.   Cf. Kuno, *op. cit.*, p. 230.
12. *Sui-shu*, ch. 3, pp. 12a and 15b.
13. 流求國, now written 琉球國.   For its history in these times,
see *Sui-shu*, ch. 81 (Tr. Pfizmaier, *op. cit.*, pp. 412–418) and *Pei-shih*,
ch. 94.   (There is some controversy as to whether the present Liu-ch'iu
Islands or Formosa is here indicated.)
14. *Sui-shu*, ch. 24, p. 18a.

sion of trade attendant on peace and prosperity within the country, led to an expansion of Chinese influence further to the west than had been possible since Han times. At the very start of his reign merchants were already traversing the "Western Regions" (Hsi-yü),[15] but there was no Chinese administration farther west than the bounds of China proper.[16] Envoys were sent out by the Emperor to various states beyond the western borders of the empire, including parts of modern Turkistan and India. They returned with lion skins, agate goblets, asbestos, dancing girls, and Buddhist sutras.[17]

With the imperial demand for "precious things" from the west came a further development of trade. The center of this exchange between the Chinese and the "barbarians" was Chang-yeh[18] in Kansu. Desirous of knowing more about these peoples and the regions whence they came, the Emperor commissioned his trusted advisor, P'ei Chü, to go to Chang-yeh to superintend this commerce and to help decide upon an imperial foreign policy.[19]

The result was that P'ei Chü wrote a geographical work[20] in which he recorded the information that he obtained from the traders concerning the geography and customs of their countries.[21]

15. 西域. This term is used for all western tribes and countries with whom China had relations, except the Western Turks. For the history of the "Western Regions" at this time see *Sui-shu*, ch. 83 (Tr. Pfizmaier, "Fremdländischen Reiche," pp. 444-477); *Pei-shih*, ch. 97; *Chiu T'ang-shu*, ch. 198; and *T'ang-shu*, chs. 221A-221B. Most of *T'ang-shu*, chs. 221A-221B, and parts of the other three *chüan* are translated by Edouard Chavannes, *Documents sur les Tou-kiue (Turcs) occidentaux*, Sbornik Trudov Orkhonskoi Ekspeditsii, No. VI (St. Petersburg, 1903), pp. 99-174. From *Sui-shu*, ch. 83, pp. 1a-1b, the part summarizing Emperor Yang's relations with the Western Regions is translated in Jäger, "P'ei Kü", pp. 220-221.

16. *Sui-shu*, ch. 67, p. 11b; *Pei-shih*, ch. 97, p. 2a.

17. *Sui-shu*, ch. 83, pp. 1a-1b, and ch. 24, p. 18a; *Pei-shih*, ch. 97, p. 2a.

18. 張掖. Commandery at modern Kan-chou 甘州; recently changed again to Chang-yeh.

19. *Sui-shu*, ch. 67, p. 10b.

20. 西域圖記 *Hsi-yü t'u-chi*, which title Jäger has translated as the "Mit Zeichnungen versehene Berichte über die Westländer," Jäger, "P'ei Kü," p. 96.

21. *Sui-shu*, ch. 67, p. 10b.

In presenting it to the Emperor he advised that the conquest of these barbarians would be an easy matter. The Emperor was much interested and personally asked about the affairs of the Western Regions. P'ei Chü was enthusiastic about the value of western trade and advised that the T'u-yü-hun²² territory which adjoined the route to Turkistan might easily be annexed.²³

P'ei Chü was then sent back to Chang-yeh²⁴ to take charge of this western diplomacy and trade. He was ordered to win over the tribes of the western border. They were to be enticed by the prospect of generous commercial profits and then persuaded to come to pay homage at court.²⁵

He was successful and from that time forward the representatives of more than thirty "states"²⁶ succeeded one another at court.²⁷ The most important were the King (*wang*)²⁸ of Kao-ch'ang²⁹ and the ruler of I-wu.³⁰ In 609³¹ when the Emperor

22. 吐谷渾, a Sien-pi (probably Mongol) tribe in the region of the present Kokonor or Ch'ing-hai. For their history see *Sui-shu*, ch. 83 (Tr. Pfizmaier, "Fremdländischen Reiche," pp. 444–452); *Pei-shih*, ch. 96, *Chiu T'ang-shu*, ch. 198; *T'ang-shu*, ch. 221A. For the pronunciation T'u-yü-hun see Pelliot's notes in *BEFEO*, Vol. V (1905), p. 429. See also his notes in *TP*, Series 2, Vol. XX (1921), pp. 323–330.

23. *Sui-shu*, ch. 67, pp. 12a–12b.

24. (About 607?)

25. *Sui-shu*, ch. 24, p. 18a; ch. 83, p. 1b; ch. 67, p. 12b; and *Pei-shih*, ch. 97, p. 2a.

26. *Kuo* 國.

27. *Sui-shu*, ch. 24, p. 18a; ch. 83, p. 1b; ch. 67, p. 12b; and *Pei-shih*, ch. 97, p. 2a.

28. *Wang* 王 is in this book generally translated as "prince" but in the cases of the *wang* of Kao-ch'ang and the *wang* of Kao-li (see Chapter V) and in the cases of rebels asserting their independence the title of "king" seems to be more appropriate.

29. 高昌, in the region of modern Turfan. For its history in these times see *Sui-shu*, ch. 83 (Tr. Pfizmaier, "Fremdländischen Reiche," pp. 454–459); *Pei-shih*, ch. 97 (Part tr. Chavannes, *Tou-kiue occidentaux*, pp. 102–103); *Chiu T'ang-shu*, ch. 198; *T'ang-shu*, ch. 221A (Tr. Chavannes, *op. cit.*, pp. 101–110).

30. 伊吾, at modern Hami. For its history in these times see *T'ang-shu*, ch. 221B, p. 14b (Tr. Chavannes, *op. cit.*, pp. 169–170).

31. *Sui-shu*, ch. 3, p. 13b. Cf. Jäger, "P'ei Kü," p. 9, n. 8. (Chavannes, *op. cit.*, p. 169, n. 8, wrongly gives 608.)

made a tour of inspection as far as the Yen-chih mountains (or hills of Yen-chih)³² beyond the Yellow River, they and the representatives of twenty-seven other states (including the T'u-yü-hun) there acknowledged his suzerainty and in turn received gifts and royal entertainment. The text reads in part as follows:

> Just before making a tour of inspection to the right [west] of the Yellow River³³ the Emperor again ordered P'ei Chü to go to Tun-huang.³³ª The latter sent envoys to Ch'ü Po-ya,³⁴ King of Kao-ch'ang, T'u-tun *shad*³⁵ of I-wu, and others to entice them by generous profits and so induce them to come to court. When, on his western inspection trip, the Emperor arrived at the Yen-chih mountains the King of Kao-ch'ang, the *shad* of I-wu, and [representatives of] twenty-seven bar-barian states³⁶ petitioned at the left side of the road. . . .³⁷

The King of Kao-ch'ang continued to be a loyal vassal of Emperor Yang. He followed the Emperor in his first campaign against Koguryŏ. Later he was honored by having a princess of imperial blood given him in marriage. The King returned home in 612.³⁸

The year 609 was one of expansion not only by trade and diplomacy but by warfare as well. The T'ieh-lo,³⁹ in spite of

32. 燕支山. East of Shan-tan 山丹 on the road to Chang-yeh in Kansu.
33. 巡河右.
33a. 敦煌. See below n. 44. P'ei Chü probably had been to Tun-huang on his previous journeys to the northwest. But I have found no reference to any such visit to Tun-huang during the preceding years.
34. 麴伯雅, reign 601-619. For the dates of Ch'ü Po-ya's reign see Lo Chên-yü, *Liao chü tsa chu* [*Miscellaneous writings in Liao*], Part II, (1933), "Kao-ch'ang Ch'ü shih nien-piao", pp. 9a-9b. Somewhat different dates are given in Huang Wên-pi, *Kao-ch'ang*, (Peiping, 1931), "Ch'ü chi" 麴紀, pp. 12b-14b.
35. T'u-tun *shê* 吐屯設.
36. 蕃胡二十七國.
37. *Sui-shu*, ch. 67, p. 13a (Tr. Jäger, "P'ei Kü", pp. 96-97). Cf. *Sui-shu*, ch. 24, pp. 18a-18b.
38. *Sui-shu*, ch. 83, p. 7b. For Koguryŏ see Chapter V.
39. 鐵勒, West Turkish tribes north of the Eastern T'ien-shan; later part of the Uigur nation. For their history see *Sui-shu*, ch. 84, and *Pei-shih*, ch. 97. See also Chavannes, *op. cit.*, *passim*, especially p. 50 n.

previous hostility to China and control over Kao-ch'ang and I-wu, were now "submissive" senders of "tribute".[40] They were persuaded by P'ei Chü to attack and defeat the T'u-yü-hun.[41] This defeat was followed up by an invasion[42] under the imperial general Yü-wên Shu[43] and the territory was then annexed by thé Chinese.

The Chinese now controlled not only Tun-huang, which P'ei Chü had termed the "throat place"—the key position on the western trade routes,[44] but, to a great extent, the main southern route through Turkistan itself. The control of ·these regions, with their trade to the west, evidently increased the imperial revenue. As the writers of those times stated the result: "Each year countless amounts of tribute were sent."[45]

This new Sui territory—some four thousand *li* from east to west and two thousand from north to south[46]—then became the scene of a great colonization project. Administrative subdivisions were set up. Lesser criminals were sent out to garrison them and to found military colonies.[47]

40. *Sui-shu*, ch. 83, pp. 4b and 8a; *T'ang-shu*, ch. 221B, p. 14b.
41. *Sui-shu*, ch. 24, p. 18b; ch. 67, p. 13a, and ch. 83, p. 4b.
42. Two different dates are given for this invasion: "Ta-yeh 4th year, 7th moon, day 32" (September 9, 608) in *Sui-shu*, ch. 3, p. 12b, and "Ta-yeh 5th year (609)" in *ibid.*, ch. 24, p. 18b. The latter date is also given in *TCTC*, ch. 181, pp. 5a–5b.
43. 宇文述, d. 616. *CCBN*, p. 240. Biography in *Sui-shu*, ch. 61; *Pei-shih*, ch. 79.
44. In his work on the Western Regions, P'ei Chü had described the three important routes traversing Chinese Turkistan from east to west and had said further: "As one knows, I-wu, Kao-ch'ang and Shan-shan 鄯善 [at present Charkhlik, south of Lop-nor] are all entrance doors to the Western Regions. Bringing together and uniting [their routes] Tun-huang is their key position [lit. throat place] . . . 敦煌是其咽喉之地." *Sui-shu*, ch. 67, p. 12a (Tr. Jäger, "P'ei Kü," p. 226).
45. *Sui-shu*, ch. 67, p. 13a.
46. See Map I. The posts farthest west were at Shan-shan and Chü-mo 且末, at present Charchan, on the southern trade route; *Sui-shu*, ch. 24, p. 18b. *Pei-shih*, ch. 97, pp. 2a–2b. Concerning this pronunciation of 且末 see Chavannes, *op. cit.*, p. 306.
47. *Sui-shu*, ch. 24, p. 18b; and ch. 83, p. 5a.

With this expansion Chinese prestige gained among the people of the Western Regions. Many of them came to the eastern capital (Lo-yang) in the winter of 609-610 and were lavishly entertained for a month. Whether or not trade opportunities afforded adequate compensation to China, is difficult to estimate. Later in the early years of the T'ang dynasty, Chinese expansion went even further and yet the historians of that time described the great expenses involved in Emperor Yang's foreign policy as an extravagance.[48]

The "barbarians" evidently were impressed with Chinese power and grandeur and the advantages of trade with the empire, for when the Emperor had his general Hsü'eh Shih-hsiung[49] take control of I-wu, P'ei Chü was able to keep the peace by announcing to the western states that it was done to facilitate trade.[50]

With I-wu, to the north, and Shan-shan, on the southern route, in his hands and with an ally at Kao-ch'ang, Emperor Yang now controlled, for the time being, the three chief routes leading from the west into China—those routes which P'ei Chü had explained to him were the lines of communication to western Asia. But these far-flung outposts were difficult to maintain even in the best of times. A stronger organization than that of the Sui was necessary to continue this extension of territory. And in the period of confusion at the end of Emperor Yang's reign, the difficulties were aggravated. "Distances by road were long drawn out, and hence it happened that robbery and seizure, death and desertion came one upon another."[51]

When troubles arose elsewhere, the Chinese were no longer able to maintain control over the T'u-yü-hun territory. Its ruler, who had formerly been expelled, returned to his domain and took advantage of the weakening of Chinese power to raid north-

48. *Sui-shu*, ch. 24, p. 18a; and ch. 67, pp. 13a-13b.
49. 薛世雄, 552-614. *CCBN*, p. 1664. Biography in *Sui-shu*, ch. 65; *Pei-shih*, ch. 76.
50. *Sui-shu*, ch. 67, p. 13b. See also ch. 65, p. 12b.
51. *Sui-shu*, ch. 24, p. 18b.

western Kansu, the region "to the right [i.e., west] of the Yellow River."[52]

In connection with these routes through Turkistan and Chinese expansion in that direction, one must also keep in mind that far more powerful neighbors—the T'u-chüeh or Turks—resided to the north and that much of China's prestige throughout Asia depended on her relation with these warlike nomads.

52. *Sui-shu*, ch. 83, p. 5a.

IV. FOREIGN RELATIONS: TURKS (T'U-CHÜEH)[1]

The ruling tribes in what are now known as Mongolia, Dzungaria, and Russian Turkistan were at this time the T'u-chüeh or Turks. Rising to power in the middle of the sixth century and exacting heavy tribute from the Northern Chou and Ch'i dynasties,[2] they were the most formidable opponents with whom the Chinese rulers of the later sixth and early seventh centuries had to deal. Nevertheless, from the commencement of the Sui dynasty, those who controlled the foreign policy of the empire succeeded in intensifying the dissension arising among various Turkish leaders over the right of succession. It is from this time on (i.e., 581) that we find a definite division between the Eastern and Western Turks.[3] The Chinese, however, were not content

1. For this pronunciation, T'u-chüeh, of the characters 突厥, see Paul Pelliot's note in *BEFEO*, Vol. V (1905), p. 429.
2. *Sui-shu*, ch. 84, p. 2b and p. 4a.
3. *Sui-shu*, ch. 51, pp. 4a, ff. Cf. Chavannes, *Tou-kiue occidentaux*, p. 260, and Stanislas Julien, "Documents historiques sur les Tou-kioue (Turcs), extrait du *Pien-i-tien*, et traduits du chinois," *Journal Asiatique*, Series 6, Vol. III (Paris, 1864), pp. 348-361.

The Eastern T'u-chüeh are also referred to as the Northern T'u-chüeh, or simply as the T'u-chüeh. For their history see *Sui-shu*, ch. 84, *Chiu T'ang-shu*, ch. 194A, and *T'ang-shu*, ch. 215A (Tr. of parts of these in Julien, "Documents historiques sur les Tou-kioue ...", *Journal Asiatique*, Series 6, Vol. III, pp. 325-367, 490–549, and Vol. IV, pp. 200-242, 391–430, 453-477 [Paris, 1864]. These translations need careful checking.) Eighth century Turkish documents dealing with Chinese intrigue against the Eastern Turks may be found in E. Denison Ross, "The Orkhon Inscriptions. Being a Translation of Professor Vilhelm Thomsen's final Danish rendering," *Bulletin of the School of Oriental Studies, London Institution*, Vol. V (1928–30), part 4 (London, 1930). See especially pp. 862 and 864. Chinese relations with the Eastern Turks are further discussed in Chapters V and VII–XII.

For the history of the Western T'u-chüeh, see *Sui-shu*, ch. 84, *Chiu T'ang-shu*, ch. 194B, and *T'ang-shu*, ch. 215A. These and other Chinese texts bearing on the history of the Western Turks are translated in

simply with two divisions but aimed constantly at undermining the power of the various leaders.

At the commencement of Emperor Yang's reign the chief of the Western Turks was Ch'u-lo Khan,[4] a powerful and self-confident ruler. His mother was Chinese. Some time before 600 she and her husband had come to the court to pay homage. She remained there and acted as an intermediary between the Chinese and her son. The Chinese were thus able to obtain from him an admission of Chinese suzerainty.[5] But in 610 Ch'u-lo refused to comply with the Emperor's request that he attend court during a western tour of inspection.[6] The Khan's followers opposed the idea. Consequently, the Emperor, upon the advice and with the aid of P'ei Chü, invested Ch'u-lo's rival Shê-kuei[7] with the title of khan and succeeded in getting him to drive Ch'u-lo out of his domain. Then, curiously enough, Ch'u-lo and some of his followers took refuge at the Chinese court,[8] and helped the Emperor in fighting against Koguryŏ.[9]

When he came to the Chinese court in 612,[10] Ch'u-lo Khan brought with him the prince Ta-nai[11] and some ten thousand men. Both of these leaders served Emperor Yang in his Korean campaigns and were honored by him in return. The Emperor desired to restore Ch'u-lo to his former power but was prevented

Chavannes, *op. cit.*, pp. 13–216, and in Chavannes, "Notes additionelles sur les Tou-kiue (Turcs) occidentaux," *TP*, Series 2, Vol. V (1904), pp. 1–110.

4. 處羅可汗, d. 619. *CCBN*, p. 1028. Chavannes, *Tou-kiue occidentaux*, No. 10 (Note: in his comprehensive work on the Western Turks, Chavannes gives a genealogical table, pp. 2-4. By reference to this and the index biographical information can easily be found.)

5. *Sui-shu*, ch. 84, pp. 15b–17a (Tr. Chavannes, *op. cit.*, pp. 14–17).

6. *Sui-shu*, ch. 84, p. 17a. Should this be the above-mentioned trip of 609? The text gives "Ta-yeh 6th year," which is equivalent to 610.

7. 射匱, (d. ca. 616). Chavannes, *op. cit.*, No. 7.

8. *Sui-shu*, ch. 84, pp. 17a–18a, and ch. 67, p. 13b.

9. See Chapter V.

10. Ta-yeh 7th year, 12th moon, day 56 (January 16, 612). *Sui-shu*, ch. 3, p. 17a.

11. *Tegin* Ta-nai 特勤大奈 (*t'ê-chin* is sometimes written *t'ê-lo* 特勒), d. after 626. Biography in *T'ang shu*, ch. 110. See Chavannes, *op. cit.*

by his own difficulties. The Turk stayed with Emperor Yang to the end of his reign. Ta-tu-ch'üeh *shad*,[12] younger brother of Ch'u-lo, remained with his flocks at Hui-ning[13] (northeast of present Ching-yüan[14] in Kansu).[15] Later, after the rebellion of Yang Hsüan-kan,[16] he was sent by P'ei Chü to raid the country of the T'u-yü-hun.[17]

Ta-nai, after participating in the Korean campaigns, distributed his hordes in Lou-fan[18] (at modern Ching-lo in Shansi)[19] and later played an important part in the T'ang campaign to gain Ch'ang-an.[20]

During this period when Ch'u-lo's group of Western Turks were giving assistance to the declining Sui dynasty, Shê-kuei Khan was ruling a land which, according to Chinese historians, extended from the Altai in the east to "the sea" in the west. As the energy of the Sui was directed towards the east in attempting the subjugation of Koguryŏ, they lost their temporary hold over the trade routes to Turkistan while the ruler of the Western Turks dominated all the little states west of Yü-mên,[21] the western limit of China proper.[22]

Shê-kuei Khan died about 616 and was succeeded by a great military leader, his younger brother T'ung Shih-hu (*jabγu*) Khan.[23] Thus the latter was reigning at the end of the Sui dynasty and the beginning of the T'ang. Never before in the knowledge of the Chinese historians had the rulers of the western barbarians been as powerful as in his time. "In the north he

12. 達度闕設. Chavannes, *op. cit.*, No. 11.
13. 會寧.
14. 靖遠.
15. *Sui-shu*, ch. 84, p. 18b; *Chiu T'ang-shu*, ch. 194B, pp. 1b–2a. (Tr. of both, Chavannes, *op. cit.*, pp. 19–21.)
16. See Chapter V.
17. *Sui-shu*, ch. 67, p. 14b.
18. 樓煩, modern 靜樂.
19. *Chiu T'ang-shu*, ch. 194B, p. 2a.
20. See Chapter X.
21. 玉門, in present western Kansu.
22. *Chiu T'ang-shu*, ch. 194B, p. 2b.
23. 統葉護可汗, d. 630 (Chavannes, *op. cit.*, p. 25, n. 3). *CCBN*, p. 1194. Chavannes, *op. cit.*, No. 8.

annexed the T'ieh-lo, in the west he fought against Persia, and in the south he became the neighbor of Chi-pin.[24]   He had hegemony over the Western Regions."[25]

Such was the empire of the Western Turks at the close of the Sui and the opening of the T'ang period.   In spite of dissension and intrigue, they were more powerful at the end of the Sui dynasty than they had been at its beginning.

24. 罽賓, in the northern part of modern Afghanistan.   Chavannes, *op. cit.*, p. 52, n. 1, and map at end of volume.

25. 霸有西域.   *Chiu T'ang-shu*, ch. 194B, p. 3a.   Chavannes, *op. cit.*, p. 24, gives the following translation: "... il eut l'hégémonie dans les contrées d'occident et les posséda."

V. FOREIGN RELATIONS AND REBELLIONS, 611-615

KOREAN CAMPAIGNS

The Chinese empire of Sui times extended into modern Manchuria as far as the Liao River. Beyond that stream, including the region of Liao-tung and part of the northern section of modern Korea, was the kingdom of Koguryŏ.[1] Packche[2] in the southwest and Silla[3] in the southeast controlled most of the peninsula but were not as powerful as Koguryŏ. The latter was the chief state of this region and played an important part in Sui foreign relations. In regard to the two lesser states, it is to be noted that on the one hand Paekche maintained an attitude of cautious friendliness towards China, offering to aid the Chinese but giving them no active assistance, while Silla sent yearly tribute to the court but was too much involved with the other states to be of any real help.

Koguryŏ, also nominally within the circle of states which acknowledged Chinese suzerainty, is noted as playing the rôle of an unsubmissive vassal and proved eventually to be an implacable enemy. Peaceful relations were maintained during most of the reign of Emperor Wên. The kings of Koguryŏ recognized China's

1. Koguryŏ (also read Ko-ku-rye). This state was also known in Korean as Koryŏ. The latter is Kao-li 高麗 in Chinese and as such is the principal form used in the Chinese texts. Chinese also: Kao-kou-li 高句驪 or 高句麗. Japanese: Kōkuli, Koma, or Kōrai. For a brief account of the history and customs of this and the other two Korean states, see Sui-shu, ch. 81 and Pei-shih, ch. 94. (Tr. of parts in Pfizmaier, "Nachrichten von den alten Bewohnern des heutigen Corea," Sitzungsber. d. k. Ak. d. Wiss. Phil.-hist. Classe, Vol. LVII, [Pai-chi] pp. 472-480, [Hsin-lo] pp. 484-492, [Kao-li] pp. 493-512.)
2. Paekche (other readings Paikche, Paik-tjyöi, and Pekshih). Chinese, principal form: Pai-chi 百濟; also Pei-chi 北濟. Japanese: Hyakusai or Kudara.
3. Silla. Chinese: Hsin-lo 新羅. Japanese: Shinra or Shiragi. (Part of Sui-shu, ch. 81, dealing with Hsin-lo is translated in Pfizmaier, "Fremdländischen Reiche," pp. 487-489.)

overlordship and sent tribute to the court; but in 597 one of these kings[4] led a raid into Chinese territory. War followed.[5]

Even though Emperor Wên's punitive campaign was unsuccessful, Koguryŏ later gave nominal submission and sent annual tribute to the court.[6] But, in 607, when Emperor Yang was inspecting his northern frontier, his loyal vassal Ch'i-min,[7] the Khan of the Eastern Turks, revealed to the Emperor that the King of Koguryŏ was in secret communication with the Turks, and thus disclosed the real hostility of that state. It was at this time that P'ei Chü's diplomacy was beginning to succeed in spreading the Chinese sphere of influence in the west. On this occasion, when Korean envoys were found at Ch'i-min's camp, P'ei Chü advised the Emperor to adopt a vigorous policy. Thereupon the latter sent the envoys back to their king to tell him that he should come to pay homage at court. "If he does not, I with Ch'i-min will certainly make a tour of inspection in his territory."[8] The Emperor asserted his right as overlord and the King of Koguryŏ had either to obey or face the consequences.

The King declined to pay personal homage to Emperor Yang and the famous campaigns which commenced in 612 were the result. In connection with the opening of hostilities, it is interesting to note other imperial activities carried on during these years. After the refusal of the King of Koguryŏ to pay homage, more than a million laborers, men and women, were put to work to construct a northern extension of the Grand Canal. The waters of the southern Ch'in River[9] were made to flow northwards away from the Yellow River to communicate with Cho-chün,[10] the

4. King Ying-yang 嬰陽王, personal name Kao Yüan 高元; reign 590–617.
5. *Sui-shu*, ch. 2, p. 12b, and ch. 81, p. 4b.
6. *Sui-shu*, ch. 81, p. 4b.
7. See p. 47.
8. Ta-yeh 3rd year, 8th moon, day 22 (September 5, 607). *Sui-shu*, ch. 3, p. 11b. (*Pi t'u* 彼土, the expression used for "his territory", indicates contempt.) See also ch. 67, p. 14a; ch. 81, p. 4b; ch. 84, pp. 14b–15a.
9. Ch'in-shui 沁水, in southeast Shansi and northern Honan.
10. 涿郡.

commandery which included the site of present Pei-p'ing.[11]   This water route[12] leading northeast from the vicinity of Lo-yang was prepared before Emperor Yang's later concentration of troops at Cho-chün.   Hence it seems to have been constructed as a means of military communication and provisioning and may be considered as an indication of the Emperor's far-sightedness in planning for the subjugation of Koguryŏ.

Meanwhile in 609, as we have seen above, Emperor Yang carried on extensive operations to the west of China.   The next year, when he was laying plans for war against Koguryŏ, he was informed by the civil authorities "that soldiers and horses were already much diminished."   Special taxes and levies were imposed at this time.[13]

By 611 the imperial canals—the new water communications linking the Yangtze valley with north China—were completed.[14] The Emperor was able to travel by boat from Chiang-tu (where he had been residing) to Cho-chün.[15]   There he assembled his troops from all over the country in readiness to start against Koguryŏ in the following year.   His plans were seriously impeded, however, by a great flood in the lower Yellow River valley which inundated over forty commanderies (*chün*).[16]   This was

11. 北平, not to be confused with the Sui commandery Pei-p'ing-chün.

12. This northern canal was called the Yung-chi-ch'ü 永濟渠.   Construction was ordered Ta-yeh 4th year, 1st moon, 1st day (day 42; January 23, 608); *Sui-shu*, ch. 3, p. 11b, and ch. 21, p. 18a.

13. *Sui-shu*, ch. 24, p. 18b.

14. A southern extension of the canal system connecting Chiang-tu with Yü-hang 餘杭 (present Hangchow 杭州 in Chekiang) was ordered put through in 610.   *TCTC*, ch. 181, p. 10b. Cf. Chi, *Key Economic Areas*, p. 118.

15. *Sui-shu*, ch. 3, p. 16b.

16. *Sui-shu*, ch. 3, pp. 16b–17a, and ch. 24, pp. 18b–19a.   The flood occurred in two general regions termed "East of the Mountains" (Shantung 山東), meaning east of the T'ai-hang Mountains (T'ai-hang-shan 太行山) of present Shansi, and "South of the [Huang-] ho" (Ho-nan 河南), meaning chiefly the area south of the Yellow River in present Honan province.

followed also by desertions among the laborers conscripted for the expedition.[17]

An actual case of desertion and the attitude of a man who soon became an important rebel leader are recorded in the following illuminating excerpt from the biography of Tou Chien-tê.[18]

> In Ta-yeh 7th year [611] there was an enlistment of men for the punishment of Kao-li [Koguryŏ]. From Tou Chien-tê's commandery[19] were selected those who were brave and outstanding to fill the posts of petty officers. And so Tou Chien-tê was put on the list as a leader of two hundred men.
>
> At this time there was a great flood "East of the Mountains". Many people were uprooted and scattered. In the same district there was a certain Sun An-tsu,[20] whose home was swept away by the flood and whose wife and children had died of hunger. The District Magistrate considering that Sun An-tsu was strong and brave conscripted him into the ranks of the army.[21] Sun An-tsu declined on the ground of poverty and spoke plainly to the Magistrate of Chang-nan.[22] The Magistrate angered had him beaten with the bamboo.[23] Sun An-tsu stabbed and slew the Magistrate and escaped to take refuge with Tou Chien-tê. Tou Chien-tê gave him shelter.
>
> In this year there was a great famine "East of the Mountains". Tou Chien-tê spoke to Sun An-tsu saying: "In the time of Emperor Wên the empire was flourishing and prosperous. He sent out a host of a million in order to attack 'East of the Liao'.[24] And yet it was defeated by Kao-li. Now that the waters have overflowed causing calamity and that the common people are poor and in distress, yet the Lord Emperor shows no consideration for their plight, but he personally

17. Ta-yeh 7th year, 12th moon (January 9=February 6, 612). *Sui-shu*, ch. 3, p. 17a.
18. 竇建德, 573–621. *GBD* 1954. *CCBN*, p. 1772. Biography in *Chiu T'ang-shu*, ch. 54, and in *T'ang-shu*, ch. 85 (Tr. Pfizmaier, "Zur Geschichte der Aufstände gegen das Haus Sui," *Sitzungsber. d.k.Ak.d. Wiss. Phil.-hist. Classe*, Vol. LXXXVIII [Vienna, 1878], pp. 782–798).
19. Ch'ing-ho-chün 清河郡, in modern southern Hopei.
20. 孫安祖.
21. 選在行中. *TCTC*, ch. 181, p. 13b, gives 選爲征士.
22. Chang-nan *ling* 漳南令.
23. In the *T'ang-shu* version of this story (ch. 85, p. 8b) Sun An-tsu is seized and punished for having stolen a sheep.
24. Liao-tung 遼東.

is marching to the Liao River.[25]   Besides, those incapacitated [lit. ulcered and sore] on account of the past years' western campaigns have not yet been recovered.   The people are reduced to extremities.   In serving the state year after year, those who went have not returned.

"Now with repeated despatches of troops[26] it is easy to cause agitation and disturbance among the people.   If we brave fellows do not get ourselves killed, we should be able to accomplish great things.[27]   Should we be only fugitive outlaws?

"I know that in Kao-chi-po[28] there is an extensive region of several hundred *li* of sedge and rushes.[29]   Relying on its inaccessible density one may there take refuge from difficulties.   If one sallies out for banditry, taking advantage of every opportunity, there would be sufficient plunder for one's maintenance.   And then, having been able to gather men about one, and keeping watch for the critical turn of events one certainly might accomplish great things [lit. have great merit] in the empire."[30]

In the succeeding years Tou Chien-tê was successful in following out this very idea himself and for some years was one of the most powerful figures in the land.

Although such desertions as this one of Sun An-tsu had occurred, there was yet no serious banditry or general disorder such as might cause modification of the imperial plans.   During the next three years (612, 613, 614) Emperor Yang campaigned against Koguryŏ.[31]

The chief feature of the campaign of 612 was the stubborn resistance of the Koreans who were besieged in Liao-tung-ch'êng

25. Liao [-ho] 遼[河], in southern Manchuria.
26. 重發兵.
27. 當立大功 (lit. should be able to do great meritorious accomplishments).
28. 高雞泊.   *Po* 泊 indicates "a boat landing".   This place was on the Grand Canal near Chang-nan.
29. 莞蒲.
30. *Chiu T'ang-shu*, ch. 54, pp. 9a–9b.   Cf. *T'ang-shu*, ch. 85, p. 8b (Tr. Pfizmaier, "Aufstände gegen Sui," pp. 782–783).   Cf. also *TCTC*, ch. 181, pp. 13b–14a.
31. For a detailed connected account of Emperor Yang's Korean campaigns see *TCTC*, ch. 181, pp. 15a–20a; ch. 182, pp. 2b–3a, and 15a–16a.

(present Liao-yang, south of Mukden).[32]   The prolonged siege of
this city exhausted the supplies of the Chinese and weakened
their morale.   After a serious defeat at the end of August,[33] the
imperial armies were forced to retreat, having been successful
only in the region west of the Liao River.   The campaign is said
to have cost several hundred thousand lives.   It was followed by
a season of drought and pestilence.   These disasters coming after
the flood of the previous year led to continued dissatisfaction
among the people of the northeastern plain, i.e., modern Shantung
and Hopei.[34]

Here then was a serious situation for the Emperor to face.   It
marks a critical point in the fortunes of the Sui dynasty.   If Emperor Yang had at this time ceased his military operations against
Koguryŏ and had made sure of internal prosperity before he engaged in any more campaigns, it seems at least possible that he
would have come nearer to establishing the magnificent empire
which he envisaged.

The T'ang authors of the *Sui History* did not hesitate to make
extreme statements about Emperor Yang's Korean policy.
While these statements may be exaggerated, they at least indicate some of the effects of the prolonged war.   To carry on these
campaigns, the Chinese government demanded forced labor,
troops, and contributions of goods and money.   These levies and
the collection of taxes are said to have been exacted in an arbi-
trary and oppressive manner, the result being that "... those
who were strong assembled and became robbers, while those who
were weak sold themselves as slaves."[35]

Emperor Yang's prestige had suffered heavily but in the next
year (613) he undertook to redeem his previous failure.   New
taxes were levied and more men were drafted to help in the line
of communication and in the armies.   By the end of March the
troops were ready and the Emperor led them himself beyond the

32. 遼東城, present 遼陽.
33. Ta-yeh 8th year, 7th moon, day 39 (August 26, 612).   *Sui-shu*,
ch. 4, p. 4b.
34. *Sui-shu*, ch. 4, pp. 1a–5b; ch. 24, p. 19a; and ch. 81, pp. 4b–5a.
35. *Sui-shu*, ch. 24, p. 19a.

Great Wall and against the towns of Koguryŏ "East of the Liao." On this occasion success seemed to be within his grasp. However, internal disorder prevented the completion of his plans.[36]

Mention has already been made of the desertions and banditry which had occurred in the preceding years. In this connection it is interesting to note what is recorded in the official annals for that period. In 608 and 609 no uprisings are mentioned. In 610 there are three notices of banditry or rebellion, and in the annals for 611 and 612 such notices are confined to what we have already mentioned concerning desertions and disaffection in the territories which had suffered from flood and through which the Korean expedition was passing.[37] But during the first part of 613[38] some seven outbreaks are recorded, five of them at P'ing-yüan, Chi-pei, and Chi-yin within the probable area of the great flood of 611.[39] One of the most serious was the plundering of horses in present northwest Kansu (i.e., beyond the Yellow River), which thus interfered with the supply of horses for the armies. A special force was sent to attempt to restore order, but without result.[40]

Yang Hsüan-kan

In spite of these signs of discontent, the Emperor persisted in his military plans and was successfully prosecuting his campaign when, in June, a serious rebellion broke out in the heart of the

36. Emperor Yang goes "East of the Liao", Ta-yeh 9th year, 3rd moon, day 15 (March 30, 613). *Sui-shu*, ch. 4, p. 6a; ch. 24, pp. 19a–19b; and ch. 81, p. 5a.

37. *Sui-shu*, ch. 3, 11b; ch. 4, p. 5b.

38. Ta-yeh 9th year, 1st to 5th moon (January 27–June 22, 613).

39. These places were all in the modern province of Shantung: P'ing-yüan 平原, about 20 miles east of present Tê-hsien 德縣 (Tê-chou 德州); Chi-pei 濟北, on the Yellow River east of present Tung-ch'ang 東昌; and Chi-yin 濟陰, northeast of present Ts'ao-hsien 曹縣.

40. *Sui-shu*, ch. 4, pp. 5b–6a. See Appendix D: Ta-yeh 9th year (613), 1st moon to 6th moon, inclusive. This appendix includes translation of items of banditry and rebellion, 613–617, from *Sui-shu*, ch. 4, and also gives the western equivalents of the Chinese dates. Cf. also *Sui-shu*, ch. 24, p. 19b, and *TCTC*, ch. 182, p. 1a.

empire. The President of the Board of Rites[41] Yang Hsüan-kan[42] revolted at Li-yang[43] and threatened the safety of the eastern capital. As soon as Emperor Yang heard of this he immediately despatched some of his best generals to suppress the uprising.[44] Thus ended the operations of 613 against the Koreans.

Yang Hsüan-kan was the son of the powerful minister Yang Su. At the beginning of Emperor Yang's reign there had been suspicion and dislike between him and Yang Hsüan-kan. The latter had thought seriously of rebelling in 609 at the time of the expedition against the T'u-yü-hun,[45] but it was not until the critical year of 613 that he found his opportunity. He then held a position of responsibility in charge of transportation at Li-yang and was able to obstruct the supplying of Emperor Yang's forces and to prepare to revolt.[46] When he did raise the standard of rebellion the Emperor was deeply involved in the Korean campaign and so far distant that it was almost a month before the news reached him.[47] The troops were at once turned back. After two months of civil war, the rebellion was put down—the leaders either killed or scattered.[48]

As far as he was able, Emperor Yang ruthlessly exterminated the party of Yang Hsüan-kan.[49] The T'ang writers recorded that "those who were killed were innumerable". They did not hesitate to attribute dire results to what they considered a policy

41. *Li-pu shang-shu* 禮部尙書.
42. 楊玄感, d. 613, *GBD* 2381. *CCBN*, p. 1260. Biography in *Sui-shu*, ch. 70 (Tr. Pfizmaier, "Fortsetzungen aus der Geschichte des Hauses Sui," *Sitzungsber. d. k. Ak. d. Wiss. Phil.-hist. Classe*, Vol. CI [Vienna, 1882], pp. 230–239) and in *Pei-shih*, ch. 41.
43. 黎陽, northeast of present Chün-hsien, Honan. Ta-yeh 9th year, 6th moon, day 42 (June 25, 613).
44. *Sui-shu*, ch. 4, pp. 6a–6b; ch. 24, p. 19b; and ch. 81, p. 5a.
45. *Sui-shu*, ch. 70, p. 1b.
46. *Sui-shu*, ch. 70, p. 2a.
47. 6th moon, day 7 (July 20, 613). *Sui-shu*, ch. 4, p. 6a. See also ch. 24, p. 19b; and ch. 81, p. 5a.
48. 8th moon, day 39 (August 21, 613); Yang Hsüan-kan defeated at Wên-hsiang 閿鄕, in Honan. *Sui-shu*, ch. 4, p. 6a.
49. *Sui-shu*, ch. 70, pp. 5a–5b; ch. 24, p. 19b. Cf. *TCTC*, ch. 18a, p. 11b.

of harsh repression. They described conditions in such exaggerated statements as the following. "People all over the empire were terrorized to the extent that nine out of ten became bandits."[50]

While Yang Hsüan-kan's forces were being attacked, another rebellion broke out, and before the end of the year there were at least eight more instances of banditry or rebellion important enough to be listed in the dynastic annals. These outbreaks occurred in widely separated parts of the empire: along the Grand Canal where it runs south of the Yangtze, in the hills of what is now central Chekiang, south of the Huai River, on the coast of present Kiangsu, along the West River west of modern Canton, in the valley of the Yellow River, and far to the west at Fu-fêng (present Fêng-hsiang, Shensi)[51] in the Wei River valley.[52] The last-mentioned outbreak was particularly significant in that the rebel leader was the first of these opponents of the Sui government to call himself "emperor".[53]

In spite of attempts at regulation, conditions went from bad to worse. The Emperor himself suffered from lack of supplies.[54] One of the first things seized by the bandits in various localities were the military horses. The insufficiency of the latter may have been partially remedied by P'ei Chü's success in getting some of the Western Turks in Kansu to raid the lands of the T'u-yü-hun.[55] Of such an alleviating factor there appears to be no mention.

The disorders and deficiencies within the empire were in part met by the government. At the same time, however, Emperor Yang continued to be guided by his ambition and to carry on the war against Koguryŏ. In 614 more troops were enlisted and the

50. *Sui-shu*, ch. 24, p. 19b.
51. 扶風, present 鳳翔.
52. *Sui-shu*, ch. 4, pp. 6b–8a. See Appendix D: Ta-yeh 9th year (613), 7th moon to 12th moon, inclusive. Cf. also *TCTC*, ch. 182, pp. 11a–13b, and 14b.
53. *Sui-shu*, ch. 4, pp. 7b–8a. See Appendix D: Ta-yeh 9th year (613), 12th moon, day 24. This date corresponds with February 2, 614.
54. *Sui-shu*, ch. 4, p. 7a.
55. *Sui-shu*, ch. 67, p. 14b. Cf. *TCTC*, ch. 182, p. 12a.

armies again sent out against the Koreans. In order to make up for the lack of horses, donkeys had to be used for transport.[56] "But now," the history tells us, "bandits and rebels arose like bees.[57] People in great numbers were uprooted to the extent of losing all connection with their homes, while communities were cut off from one another to the point of isolation. The armies in many cases failed to keep on schedule time."[58] Desertion from the ranks was punished by decapitation, but this did not prevent the evil.[59]

In spite of delays, the imperial armies did again penetrate into the territory of Koguryŏ for a third campaign and threatened P'yŏng-yang,[60] the capital of that country. On this occasion the Koreans were themselves "suffering from exhaustion"[61] and sent envoys to offer their allegiance. In Ta-yeh 10th year, 8th moon (September 9–October 8, 614), the armies were finally withdrawn.[62]

Emperor Yang, however, was still desirous that the King of Koguryŏ should himself come to court.

Again Emperor Yang demanded that the King [lit. Yüan] should come to pay homage at court. The King did not arrive after all. Hence the Emperor ordered the armies to stand by and again planned a later expedition. But at this point, the empire being in great confusion, he was therefore not able to go again.[63]

EASTERN TURKS

While Emperor Yang had been engaged in his expensive campaigns against Koguryŏ, his minister P'ei Chü was active in trying

56. *Sui-shu*, ch. 24, p. 19b; and ch. 81, p. 5b.
57. There were at least five new revolts before the end of this Korean campaign. *Sui-shu*, ch. 4, pp. 9a–9b. See Appendix D: Ta-yeh 10th year (614), 2nd moon to 6th moon, inclusive.
58. *Sui-shu*, ch. 81, p. 5b.
59. *Sui-shu*, ch. 24, p. 19b.
60. 平壤, Chinese P'ing-jang, Japanese Heijo.
61. 困弊. *Sui-shu*, ch. 81, p. 5b. See also *ibid.*, ch. 64, pp. 10a–10b; *TCTC*, ch. 182, p. 15b.
62. *Sui-shu*, ch. 4, pp. 9a–9b; ch. 24, p. 19b; ch. 81, p. 5b. *TCTC*, ch. 182, p. 15b.
63. *Sui-shu*, ch. 81, p. 5b.

through diplomacy and intrigue to weaken China's powerful northern neighbor Shih-pi,[64] Khan of the Eastern Turks.[65]   These, the original line of T'u-chüeh, had been in friendly relations with China during the reign of Ch'i-min Khan[66] (Shih-pi's father and predecessor).   Ch'i-min had with Chinese aid become chief ruler of the Eastern Turks in 603.[67]   On Shih-pi's accession in 608, he had, according to Turkish custom and with imperial consent, married a Chinese princess who had been his father's wife.[68]   In about 613, Shih-pi's tribe having become more and more flourishing, P'ei Chü attempted by various schemes either to divide or weaken his power.   Through intrigue he aimed to ruin the Khan of the Eastern Turks as he had done Ch'u-lo Khan of the Western Turks, but the result was that Shih-pi became increasingly hostile and probably discontinued appearing at court.[69]

When the campaigns against Koguryŏ had been temporarily discontinued, the Emperor made an effort to assure the allegiance of surrounding states.   At a great meeting on the first day of Ta-yeh 11th year (615), he assembled representatives of a score of different tribes and states from all directions.   These were feasted, entertained, and presented with gifts at a time when bandits and rebels were more and more weakening the empire from within.   Among Emperor Yang's guests were Turks, but it is not stated that either Shih-pi or his representatives were present at this meeting.[70]

In any case, Emperor Yang does not appear to have been

64. 始畢可汗, d. 619.   Personal name Tu-chi-shih 咄吉世.   *CCBN*, p. 551.   *Sui-shu*, ch. 84, p. 15a; *Chiu T'ang-shu*, ch. 194A, pp. 1a–2a; *T'ang-shu*, ch. 215, pp. 6a–6b.

65. *Sui-shu*, ch. 67, pp. 14b–15a.

66. 啓民可汗, d. 608.   Personal name Jan (or Jên) -kan 染干, earlier title T'u-li Khan 突利可汗.   *CCBN*, p. 897.   *Sui-shu*, ch. 84, pp. 10b–15a.   (According to *TCTC*, ch. 181, p. 7a, his death occurred in Ta-yeh 5th year [609].)

67. *Sui-shu*, ch. 84, pp. 12b–13a, and ch. 51, p. 10a.

68. *Sui-shu*, ch. 84, p. 15a.

69. See below, note 70.

70. Ta-yeh 11th year, 1st moon, day 31 (February 4, 615).   *Sui-shu*, ch. 4, p. 10a, and ch. 84, p. 15a.   The latter reference would indicate that Shih-pi came to court in this year, but according to *Sui-shu*, ch. 67, p. 15a, he ceased to come in about 613.

satisfied with the existing conditions between China and the Eastern Turks, then its most powerful neighbor. Once again he undertook a journey to the borders of his empire, this time to the north into what is now the province of Shansi.[71] It is recorded that he stayed at the Fên-yang Palace,[72] near the frontier, "in order to avoid the summer heat". But in September[73] he went out to inspect the Great Wall[74] and it seems probable that his chief aim was to secure his borders against Shih-pi Khan. The latter plotted to take the Emperor by surprise and set out at the head of some hundred thousand horsemen for this purpose. Emperor Yang was forewarned by the Chinese wife of the Turkish Khan and hastened within the walled town of Yen-mên.[75] The very next day[76] the Turks were upon him and the Emperor was here besieged for a month until relieving forces arrived and the Turks withdrew.[77]

In one account of this siege it is recorded that among the requests for aid sent out by the Emperor was a message to the same princess at Shih-pi's court who had warned Emperor Yang of the attack. She again aided the Chinese by sending Shih-pi, her husband, a false alarm of danger on his northern frontier and so caused his departure.[78]

71. Ta-yeh 11th year, 3rd moon (April 4–May 3, 615). *Sui-shu*, ch. 4, pp. 10b–11a, puts this journey in the 5th moon. But *Pei-shih*, ch. 12, and *TCTC*, ch. 182, p. 19a, agree in putting the start in the 3rd moon.

72. Fên-yang kung 汾陽宮, 160 *li* northeast of Ching-lo, Shansi.

73. 8th moon, day 2 (September 3, 615).

74. 北塞.

75. 鴈門, at present Tai-hsien 代縣, Shansi.

76. 8th moon, day 10 (September 11, 615).

77. *Sui-shu*, ch. 4, p. 11a; ch. 24, p. 20a; ch. 67, p. 15a; and ch. 84, p. 15a. Cf. *TCTC*, ch. 182, pp. 19a–20b.

78. *TCTC*, ch. 182, p. 20b. Because of similarity with other stories in Chinese history there is some reason to doubt that this gives the facts as they actually occurred. Compare the story of the Hsiung-nu siege of Han Kao-tsu and his release partly through the efforts of the Hun Empress, the *yen-chih*, in Ssŭ-ma Ch'ien 司馬遷, *Shih-chi* 史記 (ca. 99 B.C.), ch. 110. Details of the Han Kao-tsu story are given in Homer H. Dubs's translation of *The History of the Former Han Dynasty* by Pan Ku, Vol. I (Baltimore, 1938), pp. 116–117.

Another account, one which now first introduces a person of the greatest historical importance, concerns Li Shih-min, later known as the Emperor T'ai Tsung[79] of the T'ang dynasty. He was at this time fifteen years old and his father held a military command in southern Shansi.[80] Li Shih-min is said to have joined the relieving army and to have advised the general Yün Ting-hsing[81] that the best way to dispel the Turks was to extend his forces over a space of several tens of *li* and with banners by day and drums by night to make the enemy believe the relieving force to be larger than it really was. When this plan was adopted, it worked so well that Shih-pi Khan no sooner heard of their arrival than he departed.[82]

Whatever the method of his release, the Emperor, though personally unharmed, had been thoroughly frightened and re-

79. 太宗, personal name Li Shih-min 李世民, 599 (see below)-649. *GBD* 1196. *CCBN*, p. 734. Early life and reign in *Chiu T'ang-shu*, chs. 2 and 3; *T'ang shu*, ch. 2; Amiot, "Suite des Vies ou Portraits des célèbres Chinois," *Mémoires concernant l'Histoire, les Sciences, les Arts, les Moeurs, les Usages, Etc. des Chinois, par les Missionaires de Pe-kin,* Vol. V (Paris, 1780), pp. 81–189; C. Wilfrid Allan, *The Makers of Cathay* (2nd edition, Shanghai, 1925), pp. 68-80; C. P. Fitzgerald, *Son of Heaven: A Biography of Li Shih-Min, founder of the T'ang Dynasty* (Cambridge, England, 1933); and Siu Siang-tch'ou, *L'oeuvre de T'ang T'ai-tsong: Thèse pour le doctorat en droit. Université l'Aurore.* (Shanghai, 1924.)

For the date of Li Shih-min's birth *Chiu T'ang-shu*, ch. 2, p. 1a, gives K'ai-huang 18th year, 12th moon, day 55 (January 23, 599). But 600 seems to be the year as calculated from *Chiu T'ang-shu*, ch. 2, p. 1b, *T'ang-shu*, ch. 2, p. 1a, and *TCTC*, ch. 182, p. 20b. Cf. *Chiu T'ang-shu*, ch. 3, p. 20a, and *T'ang-shu*, ch. 2, p. 19b.

80. See Chapter VIII.

81. 雲定興. *CCBN*, p. 1214. Biography in *Sui-shu*, ch. 61, and *Pei-shih*, ch. 79. These give no mention of the relief of Yen-mên.

82. *Chiu T'ang-shu*, ch. 2, pp. 1a–1b. *T'ang-shu*, ch. 2, pp. 1a–1b (Confused tr. in Julien, "Docs. sur les Toukioue," III, pp. 544–545). *TCTC*, ch. 182, p. 20b. Wên Ta-ya, *Ta T'ang ch'uang-yeh ch'i-chü-chu* [*CYCCC*] (618–626. Vol. III in *Ou-hsiang ling-shih*, compiled by Miao Ch'üan-sun, 1910), ch. 1, p. 1a, mentions the siege of Yen-mên. This account includes a reference to troops recruited by Li Yüan, Li Shih-min's father (see Chapter VIII, n. 10), to help break the siege, but makes no mention of Li Shih-min's participation.

turned at once to Lo-yang.[83] This event marks a turning point in Emperor Yang's career. Heretofore he had striven, and at first successfully, to build up friendly relations with neighboring states, to extend trade, and to enlarge the empire. The Korean campaigns, however, aggravated internal distress and brought practically nothing in return for their enormous cost. And finally, at Yen-mên, the Emperor had suffered a complete loss of prestige. A "barbarian" chieftain had crossed the borders and held prisoner the "Lord Emperor" himself. From that time on Emperor Yang was on the defensive. With the keen imagination that seems to have been his, it is probable that he now realized his end was sure. Internal disorder was on the increase and there was no further attempt at foreign expansion.

In regard to the Eastern Turks, it should be noted that they long continued to be an important element in the affairs of North China. These Turks were a great power even during the time of the strong T'ang empire and not until the middle of the eighth century was their final overthrow accomplished. Even then not the Chinese but other Turks succeeded to the control of their domain.

83. *Sui-shu*, ch. 4, p. 11a.

VI. INTERNAL COLLAPSE

DISORDER AND PROPHECY, 614–616

The Sui dynastic annals for the period immediately preceding and following the siege of Yen-mên are chiefly concerned with the records of new uprisings and the government's attempts to suppress them. The year 613 had witnessed not only the great rebellion of Yang Hsüan-kan but a number of lesser revolts in other parts of the country.

About the end of that year a popular ballad or catch became current in North China and gradually assumed such importance as to warrant its later inclusion in the histories of this period.

桃李子
莫浪語
黃鵠繞山飛
宛轉花園裏

> Peach-plum Li,
> Be reserved in speech.
> As a yellow heron [you] fly round the hill
> And turn about within the flower garden.[1]

As is intended, the seditious character of this refrain emerges only on close examination. The first line identifies the subject as a man of the Li surname (meaning plum), and the second gives the meaning of the personal name Mi (secret). Li Mi[2] was

1. *Ta T'ang ch'uang-yeh ch'i-chü-chu* [*CYCCC*], ch. 1, p. 8b. This catch was sung at the time of the uprising of Li Yüan, Duke of T'ang, in 617. The first character *t'ao* (meaning peach) was interpreted as suggestive of T'ang due to the T'ao T'ang 陶唐 association in legendary history. *CYCCC*, ch. 1, pp. 8b–9a. Cf. Jas. Legge, *Chinese Classics*, Vol. III, Pt. 1, "The First Parts of the Shoo-King," p. 159.

2. 李密, 582–618 (January 20, 619). *GBD* 1176. *CCBN*, p. 418. Biography in *Sui-shu*, ch. 70; *Chiu T'ang-shu*, ch. 53; and in *T'ang-shu*, ch. 84 (Tr. Pfizmaier, "Aufstände gegen Sui," pp. 743–764). For his rebellion see below, pp. 67–69. For the connection of the ballad

one of Yang Hsüan-kan's most able assistants, who had escaped the extermination of the latter's party, and who a few years later was to lead one of the chief revolts against the Sui. The yellow heron is a bird of lofty flight, symbolic of ambition; the hill is that of Yang (i.e., the Sui);[3] and the garden represents the empire. The ballad probably originated in Li Mi's entourage and was calculated to popularize the idea of a further flight of his ambition. The catch was interpreted also as applying to other popular leaders of the name Li. The first revolt listed in the annals as occurring in the spring of 614 was one led by a certain T'ang Pi[4] at Fu-fêng, west of Ch'ang-an. This uprising, which succeeded in overthrowing the local representatives of imperial authority, is the one referred to in the preceding chapter because of its significance in that T'ang Pi did not take supreme command himself but set up a man named Li Hung[5] as "emperor" instead. It is the first instance of a Li being given that title and we may assume that T'ang Pi hoped thereby to fulfill the prophecy of the ballad.

Among other uprisings which began during the first six months of 614 two groups of bandits, one led by a man of P'êng-ch'êng,[6] in present northern Kiangsu, and the other by a man of Yen-an,[7] in present northern Shensi, were defeated by government forces. The rebels who in the previous year had seized control of the region at the southern end of the Grand Canal were also at this time finally defeated and large numbers of them put to death by the Sui official Wang Shih-ch'ung,[8] famous later as a strong rival

---

with Li Mi and its effect in gaining adherents for him in Ta-yeh 12th year (616) see Sui-shu, ch. 22, p. 24b, and TCTC, ch. 183, p. 4b.

3. See Chiu T'ang-shu, ch. 37, p. 30a, an alternative version.

4. 唐弼, Sui-shu, ch. 4, p. 9a. See Appendix D: Ta-yeh 10th year (614), 2nd moon, day 34.

5. 李弘.

6. 彭城, at present T'ung-shan 銅山 (Hsü-chou 徐州).

7. The Sui commandery of Yen-an 延安 had its capital northwest of the modern town of that name.

8. 王世充, d. 621. GBD 2222. CCBN, p. 83. Biography in Chiu T'ang-shu, ch. 54, and in T'ang-shu, ch. 85 (Tr. Pfizmaier, "Aufstände gegen Sui," pp. 766–782). For these events see Sui-shu, ch. 70, p. 10a, and Chiu T'ang-shu, ch. 54, p. 1b.

of the T'ang dynasty. But in two other widely separated places the local authorities were overthrown as they had been at Fu-fêng,—at Lang-yeh-chün[9] in the I River[10] valley of southern Shantung and at modern Foochow.[11]

In early September, 614,[12] the Korean envoys came to offer "submission". Consequently a month later, when Emperor Yang's armies were withdrawn from their war against Koguryŏ, more troops were available for use against bandits. Although Sui forces were unsuccessful against another self-styled "emperor" at Li-shih,[13] in west central Shansi, and bandits were active in the mountains of southeastern Shansi and northern Honan, yet in three other instances at the commencement of 615[14] Sui military officials were able to inflict decisive defeats upon robber bands. A group that had taken the Tu-liang Palace,[15] an imperial residence south of the Huai River, was captured by Wang Shih-ch'ung. At Ch'i-chün,[16] modern Tsinan, and in the northeast near the Great Wall, Sui generals obtained victories over rebel forces.[17]

These successes did not prevent the increase of insurrection on every side, nor did they allay the atmosphere of uneasiness and suspicion at the capital. At a time when a new group of bandits was reported as raiding to the southwest of present Pei-p'ing and allying themselves with the Eastern Turks[18] the Emperor had also to contend with intrigues and rumors at court.

During one of Emperor Yang's Korean campaigns, presumably

9. 琅琊郡.
10. I-shui 沂水.
11. *Sui-shu*, ch. 4, pp. 9a-9b. See Appendix D: Ta-yeh 10th year (614), 2nd moon to 6th moon.
12. Ta-yeh 10th year (614), 7th moon, day 1.
13. 離石.
14. End of Ta-yeh 10th year and beginning of Ta-yeh 11th year.
15. Tu-liang kung 都梁宮.
16. 齊郡, present Li-ch'êng 歷城(濟南).
17. *Sui-shu*, ch. 4, pp. 9b-10b. See Appendix D: Ta-yeh 10th year (614), 7th moon, to 11th year (615), 2nd moon.
18. *Sui-shu*, ch. 4, p. 10b. See Appendix D: Ta-yeh 11th year (615), 2nd moon, day 13.

the last one in 614, he was informed by a soothsayer,[19] of the prophecy that members of the Li family were to establish an imperial line and was advised to exterminate all of that name. This fact was then used by enemies of a prominent official, Li Hun[20] and his relative, Li Min,[21] to bring about their downfall. They and their families were executed in the spring of 615.[22]

These happenings give us some indication of the importance of the popular ballad and probably served at the time to heighten its significance among a superstitious populace. Whether or not the saying originated among the admirers of Li Mi, it encouraged the idea of rebellion in any outstanding person of the Li name. At the same time it caused the Emperor to suspect such a person. Later this situation affected the career of the founder of the T'ang dynasty.

After the execution of Li Hun and the others Emperor Yang made the journey into Shansi, that journey which ended so disastrously with his temporary imprisonment by the Turks at Yenmên. Meanwhile banditry continued in the southeastern part of Shansi and extended to the Fên River[23] valley and another robber band was formed south of the Huai.[24]

The next three months after Emperor Yang's return from Yenmên brought word of fresh rebellions. Some seriously threatened imperial communications, and some were led by men who continued to remain independent until later suppressed by the armies of the T'ang dynasty. The more important were Lu Ming-

---

19. *Fang-shih* 方士.

20. 李渾, *tzŭ* Chin-ts'ai 金才, d. 615. *CCBN*, p. 427. Biography in *Sui-shu*, ch. 37 (Tr. Pfizmaier, "Lebensbeschreibungen . . . des Hauses Sui," pp. 288-291) and in *Pei-shih*, ch. 59.

21. 李敏, 577-615. *CCBN*, p. 419. Biography in *Sui-shu*, ch. 37. (Tr. Pfizmaier, *op. cit.*, pp. 295-296) and *Pei-shih*, ch. 59.

22. Ta-yeh 11th year, 3rd moon (April 4–May 3, 615). *Sui-shu*, ch. 4, p. 10b. See Appendix D: Ta-yeh 11th year (615), 5th moon [or 3rd moon], day 34. See also *ibid.*, ch. 37, pp. 6b-8a, 11a; *Chiu T'ang-shu*, ch. 37, p. 30a; *TCTC*, ch. 182, pp. 18b–19a.

23. Fen-shui 汾水.

24. *Sui-shu*, ch. 4, pp. 10b–11a. See Appendix D: Ta-yeh 11th year (615), 5th moon [or 3rd moon] to 7th moon.

yüeh,[25] in the valleys to the southeast of Lo-yang, astride the
roads to southern China, Li Tzŭ-t'ung[26] who raided the commandery of the southern capital Chiang-tu,[27] a strong group who
resisted Sui armies in the lower Fên River valley, and Chu
Ts'an[28] who proclaimed himself "Emperor of Ch'u"[29] in the regions to the south of the Han River.[30]

The most important disorder in the first part of the next year,
616, was the invasion of the heart of Shansi by a band of some
hundred thousand men who raided the T'ai-yüan commandery[31]
from the mountains to the northeast.[32]

With uprisings and rebellions dotting the country, the conditions of the people must have been pitiable indeed. Some account of this is found in the *Sui-shu* chapter on "Food and Commodities" and presents a harrowing picture.

> At this time [the end of Ta-yeh 11th year (615)] the people abandoned
> their family homesteads to assemble within the fortifications of walled
> towns. There was nothing for them to provide for themselves. Al-
> though what was in the granaries and storehouses was still very plenti-
> ful, the minor officials[33] all feared the regulations and none dared to
> assume the responsibility of distribution of provisions for public relief.
> As a result there was increased distress. At first everyone peeled
> the bark off trees in order to eat it. Gradually they went so far as
> to eat the leaves. When bark and leaves were all exhausted they then

25. 盧明月.
26. 李子通, d. 621. *CCBN*, pp. 373–374. Biography in *Chiu T'ang-shu*, ch. 56, and in *T'ang-shu*, ch. 87 (Tr. Pfizmaier, "Zur Ge-schichte der Gründung des Hauses Thang," *Sitzungsber. d. k. Ak. d. Wiss. Phil.-hist. Classe*, Vol. XCI [Vienna, 1878], pp. 58–61).
27. Chiang-tu-chün 江都郡.
28. 朱粲, d. 621. *CCBN*, p. 263. Biography in *Chiu T'ang-shu*, ch. 56, and in *T'ang-shu*, ch. 87 (Tr. Pfizmaier, "Gründung des Thang," pp. 61–63).
29. 楚帝.
30. Han-shui 漢水. *Sui-shu*, ch. 4, pp. 11a–11b. See Appendix D: Ta-yeh 11th year (615), 10th moon to 12th moon.
31. T'ai-yüan-chün 太原郡.
32. *Sui-shu*, ch. 4, p. 12a. See Appendix D: Ta-yeh 12th year (616), 4th moon, day 60.
33. *Li* 吏.

boiled earth. Some pounded straw to powder and ate it. After this men then ate each other.[34]

It is improbable that much revenue could be derived when conditions were so bad. The flourishing western trade of earlier years was also at a standstill. In the *Sui History* section on the Western Regions we read: "Afterwards when the Middle Kingdom was in a state of anarchy, envoys and tribute were discontinued."[35] The annals for these last years of Emperor Yang's reign only once mention a foreign state sending envoys with "tribute of goods." This was the state of Chên-la[36] (in southern Indo-China), whose envoys arrived in the winter of 616,[37] an indication that China's southern trade probably was not seriously affected.

EMPEROR YANG'S WITHDRAWAL TO CHIANG-TU

In this time of confusion, after he had lost prestige and all the efforts of his former years had come to naught, Emperor Yang made matters worse when he followed the advice of those who thought primarily of his personal whims rather than the welfare of the empire. Among those whom the Emperor demoted was his father's advisor Su Wei,[38] who tried to make him appreciate the serious condition of the country. On the other hand he was much influenced by the general Yü-wên Shu, who pretended that banditry was growing less.[39]

One effect of Yang Hsüan-kan's rebellion in 613 had been the destruction of the imperial barges used by Emperor Yang in

34. *Sui-shu*, ch. 24, p. 20a.
35. *Sui-shu*, ch. 83, p. 1b.
36. 眞臘國. For its history in these times see *Sui-shu*, ch. 82 (Tr. Pfizmaier, "Fremdländischen Reiche," pp. 439–443) and *Pei-shih*, ch. 95.
37. Ta-yeh 12th year, 2nd moon (February 23–March 22, 616). *Sui-shu*, ch. 4, p. 11b.
38. 蘇威, (ca. 534–621; see *Sui-shu*, ch. 41, p. 12b). *GBD* 1790. *CCBN*, p. 1778. Biography in *Sui-shu*, ch. 41 (Tr. Pfizmaier, "Fortsetzungen . . . des Hauses Sui," pp. 188–201) and in *Pei-shih*, ch. 63.
39. *Sui-shu*, ch. 41, pp. 11b–12a. *TCTC*, ch. 183, pp. 1b–2b.

traveling along the Grand Canal.[40]   New ones were ordered and
were finished in August 616.[41]   A few days after their completion
the Emperor set out for Chiang-tu in accordance with the advice
of Yü-wên Shu.[42]   Other officials disapproved.   They voiced
strong protests right up to the time of his actual departure.   But
Emperor Yang disregarded their objections.   He even went so
far as to order the decapitation of one official who protested
against his plans.   Another, who appears to have been this official's successor, attempted to stop the Emperor on the way and
suffered a similar fate.[43]

After his withdrawal to Chiang-tu, Emperor Yang played an
insignificant part in China's affairs.   The power of government,
such as it was, fell more and more into the hands of other leaders,
officials or bandits in various parts of the country.   It is to
them and their activities that one must turn in order to understand conditions during the last two years of the Sui dynasty.

FAILURE OF EMPEROR YANG

Before going on with that phase of the story, however, it may
be well to give some tentative conclusions concerning the Emperor's personality and the disintegration of his empire.[44]   The
various factors leading to the end of the Sui dynasty together
with the political disturbances arising at that time are summarized in the concluding chapter.   Here let us briefly consider
the personal side.   What were those definite weaknesses of Emperor Yang which led most specifically to his downfall?

To begin with, we can credit the Emperor with being forceful
and imaginative.   With these qualities he went far to bring to

40. *TCTC*, ch. 182, p. 22b.
41. Ta-yeh 12th year, 7th moon (August 18–September 16, 616).
TCTC, ch. 183, p. 2b.
42. Ta-yeh 12th year, 7th moon, day 1 (August 27, 616).   *Sui-shu*,
ch. 4, p. 12a.
43. *Sui-shu*, ch. 4, pp. 12a–12b.
44. For the official summary of the Chinese historians concerning
Emperor Yang's personality and the fall of the dynasty see *Sui-shu*,
ch. 4, pp. 15a–18a, referred to above (Chapter I, pp. 9–10).

completion a conception of a magnificent empire, resplendent at home and inspiring awe abroad. Palaces, canals, fortifications, extensions of territory and foreign commerce, all these and more make us realize that Emperor Yang was a far-sighted builder, if not a genius.

But the weak side of his character seems to have overbalanced what there may have been of virtue. With his keen imagination there went suspicion. This suspicion led him to fear the designs of such diverse characters as Li Mi and Yang Hsüan-kan. He thus alienated them from him instead of making them his loyal servants as he might have done.[45]

Emperor Yang's force of character showed itself also in ruthlessness and his imagination led him beyond the bounds of practical achievement. The imposing scheme of development which he envisaged for his empire was pushed forward without regard to cost.

In planning this development, his imagination may have been caught by the sumptuous abundance of southern China as he had seen it when, as a young man, he had led Sui forces to the defeat of the Ch'ên empire.[46] Hence he attempted a luxury which was impractical in the sterner north, at least without a more powerful and extensive empire than he possessed. And it may have been partly due to his southern fancies that Emperor Yang lost the respect of some of his northern subjects.

Southern influence is noticeable in the establishment of his Yangtze capital, Chiang-tu. Mention has been made of the fact that the Emperor's final move to the south was in more than one case resisted to the death. It is further recorded that the rebellion at Chiang-tu which ended in his murder took place among a garrison of northern troops discontented at being so far from home.[47]

45. Note also Emperor Yang's execution of Li Hun and Li Min (p. 54).
46. The Empress, his wife, was also a southerner of the Hsiao family; 蕭皇后 (d. 647). See *Sui-shu*, ch. 36, pp. 7a–9a, and *Chiu T'ang-shu*, ch. 3, p. 1a, and *T'ung-chih* 通志, by Chêng Ch'iao 鄭樵 (ca. 1160), ch. 20.
47. See Chapter XI.

As to his ruthlessness, his lack of scruples in obtaining control of the empire lost him the support of several excellent officials of his father's day. And the murder of his father, if the story is to be believed, undoubtedly cost him the loyal respect of good men everywhere. Thus he weakened the empire and handicapped his own constructive efforts.

We may also attribute much of his failure to an over-aggressive attitude in his relations with neighboring states to the north and northeast. The Korean campaigns with their terrific cost in life and labor were, it seems, undertaken without regard to the strain on the empire. Moreover, Emperor Yang's relations with the Turks have a direct connection with the wars against Koguryŏ. For if, as he had boasted, he had been able to invade Korea with the aid of the Eastern Turks, the cost would not have borne so heavily on China. On the other hand, once his military strength was weakened by the first failures to subdue Koguryŏ, it seems likely that Emperor Yang was unwise in allowing P'ei Chü to continue a policy of unscrupulous intrigue among those very Turks whose friendship he should have been cultivating. The truth was that at the same time when the Emperor was being checked in the northeast and facing the serious rebellion of Yang Hsüan-kan at home, P'ei Chü was still trying to control the Eastern Turks through double-dealing. But Shih-pi Khan realized the Chinese imperialistic intentions and thus Emperor Yang alienated his most powerful neighbor. This resulted, as we have seen, in the Emperor's being besieged by the Turks at Yen-mên on his northern border.

When the imperial defences had been weakened by the Korean campaigns and Emperor Yang had suffered a complete loss of prestige at Yen-mên, the speedy collapse of his empire was inevitable.

VII. POLITICAL DISINTEGRATION AT END OF SUI PERIOD

Geographical Problem

With the collapse of centralized authority, to whom did the people turn for protection? From a glance at the map showing the spread of banditry in central and north China during the last five years of the Sui period, it will be apparent that nearly all parts of the country were disturbed and the leaders of robber or rebellious bands innumerable. In the annals many of these bandit leaders are mentioned only once, usually at the time of their first important raid or seizure of local power. Hence it is difficult to know just how many were of importance at any given time. One can only assume that, in the cases where we have no record of the leaders being subdued by the Sui authorities, the regions where uprisings had occurred continued to be rebellious towards the central government.

Biographical and chronological information concerning these rebellions is found in the Sui and T'ang dynastic histories. They present a fairly adequate picture of the situation as it existed in 617. In regard to the annals, it should be noted that the list of rebels and bandits given under Ta-yeh 13th year (617) in the *T'ang History*, as being active "at this time",[1] contains references to some men, for example Liu Yüan-chin,[2] who had been dead a year or more. The rebel Kao K'ai-tao is listed as seizing the commandery of Pei-p'ing, whereas from his biography it appears that this occurred in the following year.[3] Furthermore, Ssŭ-ma Kuang in his *Comprehensive Mirror for Aid in Government*[4] does not include this list as such and fails to mention many of these rebels in his account of the period. Nevertheless, the list has

1. 是時 ... *T'ang-shu*, ch. 1, pp. 3a–3b.
2. 劉元進.
3. See p. 66, n. 33.
4. *Tzŭ-chih t'ung-chien*

been used since it supplements in large measure the dated items in the Sui annals.

Reference has already been made to the more important uprisings which occurred up to the time of Emperor Yang's going to Chiang-tu. ⸱These will now be summarized according to their geography and additional information given concerning cases of banditry or rebellion which further disturbed the country in each locality after the Emperor's withdrawal from the north and up to the end of June 617.[5] This was the time of the most important of all the uprisings, one in T'ai-yüan in present Shansi, which later culminated in the establishment of the T'ang dynasty. The situation as it developed in Shansi will be reviewed in the next chapter.

SOUTHERN CHINA

Cut off from easy communication with the rest of the country, the regions of southern China played a minor part in the political and military events at the end of the Sui and the commencement of the T'ang dynasty. Hence in making a map designed to show the chief areas of activity at this period, the present writer has preferred to give north and central China in some detail. At the same time, it is realized that for a complete picture of the situation one must also keep in mind the regions south of the Yangtze.

Along the south and east coast of China, rebellious movements in four areas have already been mentioned: at two points on the West River, in Chien-an-chün[6] (the commandery which included the site of modern Foochow), in the hills of what is now central Chekiang, and in the old region of Wu, at the southern end of the Grand Canal. As far as is known, only the last of these uprisings, the nearest and most dangerous, but hence also the most accessible to the central authorities, was put down.[7]

After the Emperor's withdrawal to Chiang-tu, four other re-

5. Ta-yeh 13th year, 5th moon, day 1 (June 23, 617).
6. 建安郡. Present official name Min-hou 閩侯 (Fu-chou 福州).
7. See Appendix D: Ta-yeh 9th year (613), 10th moon, day 29. Rebellion suppressed in 614; *Sui-shu*, ch. 70, p. 10a, and *Chiu T'ang-shu*, ch. 54, p. 1b.

bellious movements occurred in the regions of present Kuangtung and Kuangsi. An official in Kao-liang-chün[8] in present southern Kuangtung had revolted at the time of Emperor Yang's leaving Lo-yang.[9] By the next year others in rebellion against the Sui were to be found in Yü-lin-chün[10] in present Kuangsi, in Nan-hai-chün[11] (modern Canton), and in the eastern commanderies of the Kuangtung area.[12]

Further north, but still south of the Yangtze, there are references to men who usurped imperial authority in the southern parts of present Chekiang and Anhui.[13] Of special importance was a rebellion which spread to the entire region about P'o-yang Lake[14] in present Kiangsi. By 617 this movement was led by Lin Shih-hung[15] who styled himself "Emperor of Ch'u" and who kept his power until after the beginning of the T'ang dynasty.[16]

NORTH OF THE YANGTZE

In 617 several other localities within the Yangtze valley were also the scene of insurrection against the Sui. Li Tzǔ-t'ung continued to threaten Chiang-tu from the east.[17] Tu Fu-wei,[18] another bandit leader from north of the Huai River, attacked and

8. 高涼郡.
9. *Sui-shu*, ch. 4, pp. 12a–12b. See Appendix D: Ta-yeh 12th year (616), 7th moon, day 5.
10. 鬱林郡.
11. 南海郡.
12. *T'ang-shu*, ch. 1, p. 3b. See Appendix E: Ning Ch'ang-chên, Têng Wên-chin, and Yang Shih-lüeh.
13. *Tang-shu*, ch. 1, pp. 1a–1b. See Appendix E: Wang Hua and Miao Hai-Ch'ao.
14. 鄱陽湖.
15. 林士弘, d. ca. 622. *CCBN*, pp. 580–581. Biography in *Chiu T'ang-shu*, ch. 56, and in *T'ang-shu*, ch. 87 (Tr. Pfizmaier, "Gründung des Thang," pp. 63–64).
16. *Sui-shu*, ch. 4, pp. 12b–13a. See Appendix D: Ta-yeh 12th year (616), 12th moon, day 20 and day 29. Cf. *Chiu T'ang-shu*, ch. 56, pp. 14b–15a; *TCTC*, ch. 183, pp. 6b–7a; and *T'ang-shu*, ch. 1, p. 3a.
17. *Chiu T'ang-shu*, ch. 56, p. 12a; *T'ang-shu*, ch. 1, p. 3a.
18. 杜伏威, ca. 597–624. *CCBN*, p. 461. Biography in *Chiu T'ang-shu*, ch. 56, and in *T'ang-shu*, ch. 92.

overthrew Li-yang-chün (present Ho-hsien in east Anhui).[19] They maintained their power in these regions for several years. Meanwhile to the northwest of Tu Fu-wei's position another bandit leader overthrew Ju-yin-chün (present Fou-yang, Anhui), along the road to Lo-yang.[20]

West of Tu Fu-wei's territory two outbreaks occurred in Lu-chiang-chün[21] (present Ho-fei, Anhui) during April and May. But on each occasion Sui forces gained the upper hand and suppressed them.[22] Still further west, however, in T'ung-an-chün[23] (present Ch'ien-shan, Anhui), in Yung-an-chün[24] (a commandery northwest of present Hankow), and in the region of the Yangtze gorges at Pa-tung-chün[25] (northeast of present Fêng-chieh,[26] Szechuan), rebels succeeded in holding territory in opposition to the government.[27]

In the valley of the Han River Chu Ts'an continued to be the chief figure. North of him in Nan-yang-chün,[28] Lu Ming-yüeh, who, as we have noted, had plundered the countryside of present eastern Honan, was defeated and killed by the Sui general Wang Shih-ch'ung.[29] The latter then withdrew his forces and the region was later seized by Chu Ts'an. Further up the Han other rebel armies held sway. Still another is mentioned as controlling the region where an important route crosses the mountains between

19. 歷陽郡, present 和縣. *Sui-shu*, ch. 4, pp. 12b–13a. See Appendix D: Ta-yeh 12th year (616), 9th moon, day 34, and 13th year (617) 1st moon, day 49. Cf. *TCTC*, ch. 183, pp. 10b–11a.
20. 汝陰郡, present 阜陽縣. *Sui-shu*, ch. 4, p. 14a. See Appendix D: Ta-yeh 13th year (617), 4th moon, day 34.
21. 廬江郡, present 合肥.
22. *Sui-shu*, ch. 4, p. 13b. See Appendix D: Ta-yeh 13th year (617), 3rd moon, day 55 and day 14.
23. 同安郡, present 潛山.
24. 永安郡.
25. 巴東郡.
26. 奉節縣 (K'uei-chou 夔州).
27. *T'ang-shu*, ch. 1, p. 3b. See Appendix E: Yin Kung-sui, Chou Fa-ming, and Jan An-ch'ang.
28. 南陽郡.
29. *TCTC*, ch. 183, p. 11a. See Appendix D: Ta-yeh 13th year (617), end of 1st moon.

the Han basin and Ch'ang-an.[30]   Thus the only regions of importance in the Yangtze basin which appear to have been free from serious banditry or rebellion at this time were present Hunan and Szechuan.   All one can say of them is that the annals give no record of disturbances there.[31]

THE NORTHEAST: TOU CHIEN-TÊ AND OTHERS

In northern China no region seems to have been free from rebellion.   From the tip of the Shantung peninsula to the northern bend of the Yellow River, and from beyond the Great Wall where it meets the sea to the very gates of Emperor Yang's capital at Lo-yang, men were seizing power for themselves.   On the accompanying map an attempt is made to locate these uprisings as they are recorded in the annals, the relevant parts of which are translated in Appendices D and E.   At this point the conditions in the different areas are merely outlined, only the more important of the bandits or rebels who were active in the middle of 617 being mentioned by name.

It has been noted that one of the earliest of the rebellious movements occurred in the northern part of the north China plain, within a general area "East of the Mountains", meaning east of the T'ai-hang Mountains of present Shansi.   This area continued to be the scene of banditry and the home of outlaws.   Besides those already mentioned and apart from isolated uprisings,[32] four main groups deserve our attention.

Near the mouth of the Yellow River a band of "East of the Mountains" rebels had defied imperial authority during the past four years, but Sui forces now made an active drive to suppress them.   At the end of 616 (i.e. before his campaign against Lu Ming-yüeh further south in present Honan) Wang Shih-ch'ung

30. *T'ang-shu,* ch. 1, pp. 3a–3b. See Appendix E: Yang Shih-lin, Li I-man, and Chou T'ao.
31. It is possible that the rebellion in the central Yangtze valley where Hsiao Hsien was set up as Duke of Liang may have commenced before Ta-yeh 13th year (617), 5th moon. See p. 105.
32. *Sui-shu,* ch. 4, p. 12b. See Appendix D: Ta-yeh 12th year (616), 8th moon, day 42. *T'ang-shu,* ch. 1, pp. 3a–3b.

Maybe defeated this band and killed one of its leaders. Another, the later famous contender against the T'ang, Kao K'ai-tao,[33] fled with the remainder to the northeast where he overthrew Sui authority in the region beyond the Great Wall.[34]

Two commanderies, Cho-chün, at the northern terminus of the Grand Canal, and Ch'i-chün (modern Tsinan) deserve special notice among the regions afflicted by banditry.[35] Furthermore the center of the region East of the Mountains was the scene of one of the most important rebellions of the time. Its chief had long foreseen the ending of the Sui dynasty and was now among the more significant leaders to declare his independence of Sui rule. This rebel was Tou Chien-tê.

We have noted his plan for becoming a bandit leader in the early days of Emperor Yang's campaigns against Korea and also that several others had from time to time seized power in the lower Yellow River valley. In 616 Chang Chin-ch'êng[36] was the most important rebel leader in that region. When he was overthrown, his followers turned to another named Kao Shih-ta.[37] Tou Chien-tê, because of sympathy with the outlaws, had been forced to flee and had joined Kao Shih-ta. When the latter failed to make use of Tou Chien-tê's talents and was himself defeated and slain by Sui forces, Tou Chien-tê remained as the most prominent figure in the region.[38]

By the end of 616 he and his followers controlled an area in northeast China extending from the region of Kao-chi-po in the

33. 高開道, d. 624. *CCBN*, p. 887. Biography in *Chiu T'ang-shu*, ch. 55, and in *T'ang-shu*, ch. 86 (Tr. Pfizmaier, "Gründung des Thang," pp. 34–38).

34. *TCTC*, ch. 183, pp. 7a–9b. See Appendix D: Ta-yeh 12th year (616), 12th moon (end). Cf. *Chiu T'ang-shu*, ch. 55, p. 12b.

35. *T'ang-shu*, ch. 1, p. 3a, and *TCTC*, ch. 183, pp. 9b–10a.

36. 張金稱, d. 616 (*TCTC*, ch. 183, p. 8a). See Appendix D: Ta-yeh 9th year (613), 10th moon, day 29; 11th moon, day 46; and 12th year (616), 12th moon.

37. 高士達, d. 616 (*Chiu T'ang-shu*, ch. 54, p. 11a). See Appendix D: Ta-yeh 9th year (616), 12th moon.

38. *Chiu T'ang-shu*, ch. 54, pp. 10a–11b; *T'ang-shu*, ch. 85, pp. 9a–10a.

lower Yellow River valley to the mountains west of present Pei-p'ing.[39] Tou Chien-tê was at the head of some hundred thousand men, including many former Sui officials.[40] By the middle of February 617[41] he felt himself powerful enough to assume the title of King (*wang*), with his capital at Lo-shou, in Ho-chien-chün.[42] He continued to be an important contender for power in the empire until as late as 621.

Li Mi

To the southwest of Tou Chien-tê and upstream along the Yellow River valley was perhaps the most serious of the various rebellions which threatened the existence of the Sui dynasty. The region in the vicinity of Lo-yang had been the scene of Yang Hsüan-kan's uprising. Now, one of the latter's associates, Li Mi, took advantage of the Emperor's withdrawal to Chiang-tu to gain much of the territory for himself.

We have noted popular uprisings in many parts of the country, as shown for instance in the discontent of Tou Chien-tê and his friends. In the case of Li Mi, however, a member of the higher classes revolted and helped to lead the opposition to Emperor Yang. His rebellion takes on added significance on that account.

Li Mi was a descendant of men who had been distinguished in official life. As a youth he had himself held a position in the palace guard, but found it prudent to retire when Emperor Yang took a dislike to his looks. Thereupon he became a diligent student of military history and thus won the attention of Yang Su and his son Yang Hsüan-kan.[43] The latter called Li Mi to his

39. Seizure of Jao-yang 饒陽 and move to P'ing-yüan; *Chiu T'ang-shu*, ch. 54, p. 11b. Seizure of Wei Tao-êrh's territory; *T'ang shu*, ch. 85, p. 10a. For Wei Tao-êrh see below p. 79, n. 45.

40. *Chiu T'ang-shu*, ch. 54, p. 11b; *T'ang-shu*, ch. 85, p. 10a.

41. Ta-yeh 13th year, 1st moon (February 11–March 12, 617).

42. 樂壽, in 河間郡. *Chiu T'ang-shu*, ch. 54, p. 11b; and *T'ang-shu*, ch. 1, p. 3a, and ch. 85, p. 10b. *Chiu T'ang-shu*, ch. 1, p. 5b, gives I-ning 義寧 2nd year, 2nd moon (March 2–31, 618) as date of his assumption of title of *wang*.

43. *Chiu T'ang-shu*, ch. 53, pp. 1a and 1b. *T'ang-shu*, ch. 84, pp. 1a–1b.

aid in 613 and Li Mi was one of his advisors during the ill-fated rebellion of that year.[44]

From then on Li Mi was a fugitive from the Sui authorities. At this time the popular ballad which foretold success for one of the Li name became current and played an important rôle in giving additional prestige to such men as Li Mi. It seems likely that the catch originated among his followers and gave him especial prominence as a rival for power in the empire from 613 until the time of his death.

In about 616 Li Mi offered his talent to Ti (or Chai) Jang,[45] bandit leader of Tung-chün on the Yellow River, scene of an unsuccessful uprising of 613.[46] Ti Jang had already collected a following of some ten thousand men. On Li Mi's advice they attacked and defeated Sui troops in Jung-yang-chün[47] east of Lo-yang, in the autumn of 616.[48]

Li Mi soon became the real leader of the band and began a series of operations which added to his popularity among the people. He directed his campaigns against those imperial storehouses or granaries which were such an important part of the Sui economic system. In March 617,[49] a surprise attack was made on the Hsing-lo Granary. This was then opened for the benefit of the people.[50] Furthermore, the army of some twenty-five thousand which was sent against Li Mi from Lo-yang was defeated, an achievement which added to his prestige. He set himself up as an independent ruler with the title of Duke of Wei,[51]

44. *Chiu T'ang-shu*, ch. 53, pp. 1b–3b. *T'ang-shu*, ch. 84, pp. 1b–3a.
45. 翟讓. Some biographical information in Li Mi's biographies. See Chapter VI, n. 2.
46. 東郡. *Sui-shu*, ch. 4, p. 7a. See Appendix D: Ta-yeh 9th year (613), 10th moon, day 14.
47. 榮陽郡, present Chêng-hsien 鄭縣 (Chêngchow 鄭州). Alternative pronunciation: Ying-yang-chün.
48. Ta-yeh 12th year, 10th moon (November 15–December 13, 616). *Chiu T'ang-shu*, ch. 53, p. 4b; *T'ang-shu*, ch. 84, p. 3b. Cf. *TCTC*, ch. 183, pp. 3b–6b.
49. Ta-yeh 13th year, 2nd moon, day 27 (March 21, 617).
50. *Chiu T'ang-shu*, ch. 53, p. 3b. Cf. *Sui-shu*, ch. 4, p. 13b. See Appendix D: Ta-yeh 13th year (617), 2nd moon, day 27 and day 37.
51. 魏公.

a hierarchy of officials beneath him and his capital at Kung,[52] near the mouth of the Lo River. "His host reached several thousand. All the commanderies 'South of the [Yellow] River' were in turn overthrown by him".[53]

In May of the same year another storehouse, the Hui-lo Granary, was seized,[54] and one of Li Mi's subordinates raided the suburbs of the eastern capital itself. Other rebels, including Sui officials to the south at Huai-yang-chün[55] (present Huai-yang-hsien, Honan) joined his forces.

Strenuous fighting was necessary in order to attain this degree of success. And in spite of his large following Li Mi failed in his attempts to take Lo-yang.[56] Nevertheless his insurrection was probably the most outstanding at this time and certainly constituted the gravest threat to the center of Sui power at Lo-yang.

THE NORTHWEST: HSIEH CHÜ AND OTHERS

To the west of T'ung-kuan, the important pass at the elbow of the Yellow River which has been termed "the gateway of central Asia",[57] we come to Kuan-chung,[58] the "Region within the Passes", and further on to the mountains of modern Kansu. In these parts scattered outbreaks had occurred prior to Emperor Yang's withdrawal to Chiang-tu in 616.

The one rebellious group which continued to be of importance

52. 鞏.

53. *Sui-shu*, ch. 4, p. 13b. See Appendix D: 2nd moon, day 37. See also *Chiu T'ang-shu*, ch. 53, p. 5b; *T'ang-shu*, ch. 1, p. 3a, and ch. 84, pp. 4a–4b.

54. Ta-yeh 12th year, 4th moon, day 30 (May 23, 617). *Sui-shu*, ch. 4, p. 14a, gives Hui-lo tung-ts'ang 迴洛東倉. See Appendix D: Ta-yeh 13th year (617), 4th moon, day 30.

55. 淮陽郡.

56. *Sui-shu*, ch. 4, p. 14a. See Appendix D: Ta-yeh 13th year (617), 4th moon, day 26, day 30, and "In this moon. . . ." *Chiu T'ang-shu*, ch. 53, p. 6a. *T'ang-shu*, ch. 84, p. 5a.

57. George Babcock Cressey, *China's Geographic Foundations: A Survey of the Land and Its People* (New York, 1934), p. 197.

58. 關中, present Shensi north of the Ch'in-ling 秦嶺 Mountains.

was directly beyond the western capital, Ch'ang-an. At Fu-fêng-chün, T'ang Pi and his nominal "emperor", Li Hung, had controlled the commandery for the past three years.[59]　In the same year in which the Emperor left the north, however, one rebel seized power in P'ing-i-chün[60] near the elbow of the Yellow River, and another at Lin-ching[61] in the highlands of present eastern Kansu.[62]　The records for the next year indicate that two other groups seized power in this vicinity, one at Hung-hua-chün[63] to the east and another in the Ching River[64] valley to the south.[65]

To the north the Assistant Commandery Administrator[66] at Shuo-fang-chün[67] in the Ordos was killed and his commandery seized by a rebel named Liang Shih-tu.[68]　The latter also defeated a Sui general sent to oppose him. He and another rebel leader, further north at Yü-lin, were in close touch with the Eastern Turks and in about April received titles at the hands of

59. T'ang Pi was still in power in Fu-fêng when Hsieh Chü invaded it in 617; see p. 106. This conflicts somewhat with an item in the T'ang-shu list of rebels, (ch. 1, p. 3a). A man named Shao Chiang-hai 邵江海 is said to have "seized Ch'i-chou 岐州" at this time (see Appendix E). Ch'i-chou was an early Sui name and a T'ang name for Fu-fêng-chün. It is possible that T'ang Pi was at Ch'ien-yüan-hsien 汧源縣 and that Shao Chiang-hai was at Yung-hsien 雍縣, the commandery seat. But this does not seem probable, since Shao Chiang-hai is not mentioned in the accounts of Hsieh Chü's attack on Fu-fêng-chün. He is not included in the CCBN. This one note is the only reference to him which I have found.

60. 馮翊郡, present Ta-li-hsien 大荔縣, Shensi.

61. 臨涇.

62. Sui-shu, ch. 4, pp. 12a–12b. See Appendix D: Ta-yeh 12th year (616), 7th moon, day 5, and 9th moon, day 59.

63. 弘化郡, present Ch'ing-yang 慶陽. Sui-shu, ch. 4, p. 13a. See Appendix D: Ta-yeh 13th year (617), 1st moon, day 18.

64. Ching-shui 涇水.

65. T'ang-shu, ch. 1, p. 3a. See Appendix E: Tso Nan-tang.

66. Chün-ch'êng 郡丞.

67. 朔方郡.

68. 梁師都, d. 628. CCBN, p. 998. Biography in Chiu T'ang-shu, ch. 56, and in T'ang-shu, ch. 87 (Tr. Pfizmaier, "Gründüng des Thang", pp. 66–69).

Shih-pi Khan.[69]   In the northwestern Ordos a Sui commandery official[70] of Wu-yüan-chün[71] also adhered to the Turks and received a title from them.[72]

In northwestern China as a whole the most important rebellion at this time was that of Hsieh Chü,[73] an official[74] of Chin-ch'êng-chün[75] [present Kao-lan (Lanchow) in Kansu], where the main routes to Central Asia cross the Yellow River.   At a time when troops were being raised to oppose bandits he revolted against the magistrate, imprisoned all the local officials and in May, 617, proclaimed his independence as King Lord Protector of Western Ch'in.[76]   Soon thereafter Hsieh Chü succeeded in gaining control of the neighboring commanderies, including Pao-han-chün[77] to the southwest, Hsi-p'ing-chün and Chiao-ho-chün[78] to the northwest, and Lung-hsi-chün[79] at the headwaters of the Wei River to the southeast.   As long as he held Lung-hsi-chün he was in a position to threaten the western capital itself.[80]

In spite of the growing power of Hsieh Chü to the west of

69. *Sui-shu*, ch. 4, p. 13a, and *TCTC*, ch. 183, pp. 11a, 14a–14b. See Appendix D: Ta-yeh 13th year (617), 2nd moon, day 19, and 3rd moon, day 4.   See also quotation, p. 92.

70. *T'ung-shou* 通守.

71. 五原郡.

72. *T'ang-shu*, ch. 1, p. 3a.   See Appendix E: Chang Ch'ang-hsün. 張長遜, d. 637.   *CCBN*, p. 941.   Biography in *Chiu T'ang-shu*, ch. 57, and in *T'ang shu*, ch. 88 (Tr. Pfizmaier, "Gründung des Thang," pp. 99-100).

73. 薛舉 (the name 薛 is also often pronounced Hsüeh), d. 618. *CCBN*, p. 1672.   Biography in *Chiu T'ang-shu*, ch. 55, and in *T'ang-shu*, ch. 86 (Tr. Pfizmaier, "Aufstände gegen Sui," pp. 799-803).

74. *Hsiao-wei* 校尉.

75. 金城郡, present 皇蘭 (Lan-chou 蘭州).

76. 西秦霸王.

77. 枹罕郡.

78. 西平郡 and 澆河郡, referred to as Shan-chou 鄯州 and K'uo-chou 廓州 respectively.

79. 隴西郡.

80. *Sui-shu*, ch. 4, p. 13b.   See Appendix D: Ta-yeh 13th year (617), 4th moon, day 20.   *Chiu T'ang-shu*, ch. 55, pp. 1a–2a.   *T'ang-shu*, ch. 1, p. 3a, and ch. 86, pp. 1a–1b.

Ch'ang-an and of Li Mi to the east of Lo-yang and of the fact that Emperor Yang was far away at Chiang-tu, these two capitals, the territory between them and much of the region of modern Shansi to the north of it were still loyal to the Sui Emperor. There were also other regions which remained faithful to the dynasty. From the above description, however, it appears that few sections or lines of communication of importance in the country remained which had not suffered or were not now disturbed by banditry and rebellion.

VIII. SHANSI: IMPORTANCE OF LI YÜAN[1]

SHANSI, 614–616

In considering political conditions as they developed in the Sui empire after Emperor Yang's withdrawal to Chiang-tu, attention has already been drawn to various sections of the country, because of their geographical importance or the strong leaders who secured partial or complete independence at this time. The situation as it was developing in the region which now comprises the province of Shansi is important from both points of view.

We have seen that this region, like most parts of China, was in these years affected by roving bands of outlaws. Especially in the highlands east and west of the Fên River valley was this the case. At Li-shih-chün, about eighty miles west of T'ai-yüan,[2] a rebellious group as early as 614 had held out against Sui forces.[3] In the following year another band had come through the mountains of the southeast from the region of Ch'ang-p'ing-chün[4]

1. In this and the succeeding chapters the historical narrative is largely based on the standard dynastic histories, principally the *Chiu T'ang-shu*. In the latter the account of Li Yüan's rise to power differs in many significant details from the account given in the *Ta T'ang ch'uang-yeh ch'i-chü-chu* [*CYCCC*]. The present writer realizes the importance of this work (see notes in Bibliography) and is undertaking a special study concerning the points of difference between the *CYCCC* and the official histories. It is here intended to give merely a simple outline of the events at the founding of the T'ang dynasty and to show as clearly as possible the position of Li Yüan in relation to the general situation throughout the country. Many specific details taken from the *Chiu T'ang-shu* will probably need revision in the light of further research in the *CYCCC* and are to be accepted only as representing the official standard account.

2. 太原, alternative name for T'ai-yüan-chün; see p. 130, n. 2.

3. *Sui-shu*, ch. 4, pp. 9b–10a. See p. 53, and Appendix D: Ta-yeh 10th year (614), 11th moon, day 52.

4. 長平郡.

73

(northeast of modern Chin-ch'êng[5]) to raid one of the commanderies of the Fên valley, Hsi-ho-chün (present Fên-yang
[Fênchow]).[6] It was in this year that Emperor Yang was be-
leaguered at Yen-mên in the north of the present province. After
his withdrawal from the region, the imperial forces became involved with a new group of rebels[7] in the lower Fên valley at
Chiang-chün.[8] Still others, as we have seen, came from the
northeast to raid T'ai-yüan-chün in 616. Thus the weakening of
Sui authority was particularly evident in the territory of Shansi.

To the north of this region lay the domain of the nomads, then
controlled by China's most powerful neighbor, Shih-pi Khan of
the Eastern Turks. He and his forces had besieged the Emperor
in 615. The raiders of T'ai-yüan were his allies and in 616, when
the Sui decline was increasingly apparent, he invaded the borders
again.[9] But on this occasion Shih-pi did not find the Sui armies
as weak as before. An officer who had seen years of military
service was in command in southern Shansi and played an important part in checking the advance of the Eastern Turks.
This was Li Yüan, Duke of T'ang (posthumously known as Kao-
tsu),[10] who was soon to become the first emperor of the T'ang
dynasty.

To understand events as they developed in Shansi, we must go
back to trace the career of the Duke of T'ang and his share in
those happenings which have just been described.

5. Chin-ch'êng-hsien 晉成縣 (Tsê-chou 澤州).
6. 西河郡, present 汾陽 (Fên-chou 汾州). Sui-shu, ch. 4, pp. 9b,
10b. See p. 54, and Appendix D: Ta-yeh 11th year (615), 5th moon
[or 3rd moon], day 40.
7. Ch'ai Pao-ch'ang 柴保昌, etc. Sui-shu, ch. 4, p. 11b. See Appendix D: Ta-yeh 11th year (615), 12th moon, day 17.
8. 絳郡, modern Chiang-chou 絳州.
9. Sui-shu, ch. 84, p. 15a; T'ang-shu, ch. 1, p 2a. See below, p. 130.
10. 高祖, inherited title Duke of T'ang 唐公, personal name Li
Yüan 李淵, 566–635. GBD 1239. CCBN, p. 738. Early life and
reign in Chiu T'ang-shu, ch. 1; T'ang-shu, ch. 1 (part tr. in Pfizmaier,
"Aufstände gegen Sui," pp. 729–743); Amiot, "Portraits des célèbres
Chinois," Mem. conc. les Chinois, Vol. V, pp. 80–124. For a detailed
history of his activities from 615 to 618 see CYCCC, passim.

LI YÜAN

Li Yüan was born of a noble family at Ch'ang-an in 566.[11] His father, Li Ping,[12] was Military Commander of An-chou and State Pillar Generalissimo[13] under the Northern Chou dynasty and had succeeded to the title of Duke of T'ang, which had been created to commemorate the services of Li Ping's father by the founder of the Chou dynasty.[14] Li Yüan's mother[15] was a member of the Tu-ku family and a sister of the Empress of the Sui Emperor Wên.[16] When Li Yüan was only six years old, he inherited the title of Duke of T'ang.[17]

From the beginning of the Sui period he held official positions under the dynasty. In the annals, Li Yüan is referred to by his temple name, Kao-tsu.

When the Sui ascended the throne, he was honored by an appointment in the *ch'ien-niu pei-shên* [a palace guard].[18]

The Sui Emperor Wên's Empress of the Tu-ku family was the aunt of Kao-tsu. On that account he enjoyed special favors on the part of Emperor Wên. He was promoted to be the Prefect[19] of the three prefectures of Ch'iao, Lung, and Ch'i[20] in succession . . .

11. *Chiu T'ang-shu,* ch. 1, pp. 1a–1b.
12. 李昞, (d. 572. See *Chiu T'ang-shu,* ch. 1, pp. 1a–1b). *CCBN,* p. 407.
13. An-chou *tsung-kuan chu-kuo ta-chiang-chün* 安州總管柱國大將軍. An chou was at present Mi yün hsien 密雲縣 in northern Hopei.
14. *Chiu T'ang-shu,* ch. 1, pp. 1a–1b. Note *T'ang-shu,* ch. 1, p. 1b, gives Li Ping as holding these offices under the Sui dynasty and is evidently wrong if he died in 572. (See above, n. 12.)
15. Empress Yüan-chên 元貞皇后. This was a posthumous title given her as the mother of the first T'ang emperor.
16. See below and see biography of her father Tu-ku Hsin in *CCBN,* p. 1587. See also *Chou-shu,* ch. 16, and *Pei-shih,* ch. 61, p. 4a.
17. *Chiu T'ang-shu,* ch. 1, p. 1b.
18. 千牛備身.
19. *Tz'ŭ-shih* 刺史.
20. 譙隴岐三州. Ch'iao-chou was in northern Anhui; Sui: Shansang-hsien 山桑縣. Lung-chou was in Shensi; Sui: Ch'ien-yüan-hsien. For Ch'i-chou see Chapter VII, n. 59.

At the beginning of the Ta-yeh period [605–617] he was Commandery Administrator[21] of the two commanderies of Jung-yang and Lou-fan.[22] He was summoned to the post of Assistant Supervisor in the Administration of the Imperial Domestic Service.[23]

In the 9th year of Ta-yeh [613] he was transferred to be Vice-President of the Court of Imperial Insignia.[24] During the Liao-tung campaign [i.e. the campaign against Koguryŏ] he superintended the transport [of provisions][25] at Huai-yüan-chên.[26] When Yang Hsüan-kan rebelled, Emperor Yang instructed Kao-tsu to ride posthaste to guard Hung-hua-chün and to take charge of all the armies to the right of the pass.[27]

Kao-tsu continuously served in palace and provincial posts and made himself known as a kind and upright man. At this time, moreover, those "brave gentlemen",[28] whom he had succeeded in binding to himself, flocked to him in increasing numbers.[29]

It was during these years, as we have seen, that Emperor Yang was waging his exhausting campaigns against Korea while banditry and disaffection increased throughout the empire. Then there arose the popular ballad prophesying great things for those of the Li name. Li Hun and his relatives were the chief sufferers from this rumor, but any outstanding person named Li, such as Li Yüan, was naturally under a cloud of suspicion and would take care to keep out of reach as much as possible.

The T'ang annals tell us:

At this time there were many who were suspected and disliked by Emperor Yang.[30] [On this account he executed great ministers with

21. *T'ai-shou* 太守.
22. Lou-fan-chün 樓煩郡, present Ching-lo 靜樂, in northern Shansi.
23. *Tien-nei shao-chien* 殿內少監.
24. *Wei-wei shao-ch'ing* 衛尉少卿.
25. Supplied from *T'ang-shu*, ch. 1, p. 1b.
26. 懷遠鎮, north of Liao-hsi-chün 遼西郡 in present southwestern Manchuria.
27. Kuan-yu 關右. The exact location of these armies is uncertain.
28. *Hao-chieh* 豪傑.
29. *Chiu T'ang-shu*, ch. 1, pp. 1b–2a. Cf. *T'ang-shu*, ch. 1, p. 1b, and *TCTC*, ch. 182, pp. 10b–11a.
30. *Chiu T'ang-shu*, ch. 1, p. 2a.

their whole families.[31]] Just then there was an edict summoning Kao-tsu to the place where the Emperor was. Kao-tsu happened to be ill and delayed his appearance. At this time Kao-tsu's sister's daughter, the Lady Wang,[32] being in the women's apartments of the palace, the Emperor questioned her saying: "Why is your uncle late?" The Lady Wang replied that it was on account of illness. The Emperor said: "I wonder if he is courting death?"

When Kao-tsu heard this he feared more and more; hence he gave way to drink and led an [apparently] dissolute life [lit. sank flushed with drink] and gave bribes seeking thereby to disguise his conduct.[33]

Thus we see that while the Duke of T'ang was closely connected with the imperial house and had apparently been a loyal public servant from the beginning of the Sui dynasty, yet his bearing the Li name, his position, and his popularity served to alienate him from Emperor Yang.

DEFEAT OF BANDITS AND TURKS, 615–616

Nevertheless the Sui empire was in dire need of loyal officials. In 615, when Emperor Yang was in Shansi, he was not far from where rebellious groups were holding out against imperial authority in the highlands on both sides of the Fên River valley. Hence the Emperor appointed the Duke of T'ang as a special commissioner, "Legate Pacifical" of Ho-tung (present Yung-chi [P'u-chou]),[34] with extraordinary powers to restore order in that region.[35] This Li Yüan succeeded in doing by defeating two bandit groups, both in the lower Fên valley. Through his personal bravery he checked the attack of Mu Tuan-êrh[36] at Lung-mên[37] and, in the next year, he forced the surrender of the Chiang-

31. Supplied from *T'ang-shu*, ch. 1, p. 1b.
32. 王氏. Literally "Lady of Clan Wang."
33. *Chiu T'ang-shu*, ch. 1, p. 2a. Cf. *T'ang-shu*, ch. 1, pp. 1b–2a, and *TCTC*, ch. 182, p. 11a.
34. Ho-tung *wei-fu ta-shih* 河東慰撫大使. Ho-tung-chün was at present Yung-chi-hsien 永濟縣 (P'u-chou 蒲州).
35. *T'ang-shu*, ch. 1, p. 2a; *Chiu T'ang-shu*, ch. 1, p. 2a; and *TCTC*, ch. 182, p. 19a. *TCTC* gives *fu-wei ta-shih* for this title.
36. 毋端兒. It is possible that this should be Wu Tuan-êrh 毋端兒.
37. 龍門, near the mouth of the Fên River.

chün bandit leader, Ch'ai Pao-ch'ang, who had long held out against Sui authority and whose several tens of thousands of men were now brought to submit.[38]

In the same year in which he gained the submission of the bandits at Chiang-chün, the Duke of T'ang was promoted to be General of the Right Brave Guard.[39]   His next task was to resist the advance of the Turks.

Shih-pi Khan's line of attack into Shansi lay through the frontier commandery, Ma-i-chün[40] (modern Shuo-hsien). Li Yüan, therefore, hastened to join the Administrator of this commandery, Wang Jên-kung,[41] in opposing the Turkish advance. This is the account of the events as they are recorded in the annals of the *New T'ang History:*

> The Turks invaded the frontier. Kao-tsu and Wang Jên-kung, Commandery Administrator of Ma-i, attacked them. But the Sui troops being few were no match for them.   Hence Kao-tsu chose two thousand picked cavalry as a "Roving Army" which were to camp and provision with regard to the streams and grasslands as do the Turks and which were also to [spend their time] hunting and racing to show that they were taking their leisure.   On the other hand he selected skilled bowmen and kept them in ambush as special troops.   Observing Kao-tsu the enemy were suspicious and did not dare to engage in battle. Kao-tsu took the opportunity and attacked them. The Turks were defeated and fled.[42]

Meanwhile Sui forces had been defeated in T'ai-yüan, in the heart of Shansi.   The situation demanded the Duke of T'ang's attention if Sui power was to be maintained.   Chên Ti- (or Chai-)êrh,[43] subordinate commander under an ally of the Turks, had swept into this region with a hundred thousand men and had

38. *Chiu T'ang-shu,* ch. 1, p. 2a; *T'ang-shu,* ch. 1, p. 2a.
39. *Yu-hsiao-wei chiang-chün* 右驍衛將軍. *Chiu T'ang-shu,* ch. 1, p. 2a.
40. 馬邑郡, present Shuo-hsien 朔縣, in northern Shansi.
41. 王仁恭, 558–617. *CCBN,* p. 79.   Biography in *Sui-shu,* ch. 65, and in *Pei-shih,* ch. 78.
42. *T'ang-shu,* ch. 1, p. 2a.   Cf. *Sui-shu,* ch. 84, p. 15; and *TCTC,* ch. 183, pp. 10a–10b.   *TCTC* puts this campaign against the Turks after the defeat of Chên Ti-êrh (see below).
43. 甄翟兒.

successfully resisted the Sui general who had been sent to suppress him.[44]   It was against this bandit leader that the Duke of T'ang now turned his efficient forces. "Ta-yeh . . . 12th year . . . 12th moon . . . day 29 [January 22, 617]. . . . The Duke of T'ang defeated Chên Ti- [or Chai-]êrh at Hsi-ho. He took prisoner several thousand men and women."[45]

PREËMINENCE IN SHANSI

This battle assured the Duke of T'ang's preëminence in Shansi. Having defeated bandits in the south and Turks in the north, he was now also master of the central and most important commandery of the modern province, T'ai-yuan-chün. Soon thereafter, in 617, the Duke of T'ang became the Garrison Commander of T'ai-yüan.[46]

Whether or not this appointment, as recorded in some of the sources, was made before the defeat of Chên Ti-êrh is probably of little consequence.[47]   Chiang-tu was almost completely cut off

44. *Sui-shu*, ch. 4, pp. 10b, 12a. See Appendix D: Ta-yeh 12th year (616), 4th moon, day 60.

45. *Sui-shu*, ch. 4, p. 13a.   *TCTC*, ch. 183, p. 7a, also gives 12th year (616), 12th moon, and mentions Chên Ti-êrh. In the biographies of Li Shih-min, *Chiu T'ang-shu*, ch. 2, pp. 1b–2a, and *T'ang-shu*, ch. 2, p. 1b, we read of his taking an important part in the battle. Both of these and *T'ang-shu*, ch. 1, p. 2a, and *CYCCC*, ch. 1, pp. 2a–2b, indicate Ta-yeh 13th year (617) as the date of the battle. The *Chiu T'ang-shu*, ch. 2, version refers to the bandit leader in this case as Wei Tiao-êrh (or Tao-êrh) 魏刁兒 (or 刀兒), styled Li-shan-fei 歷山飛, who the *Sui-shu* informs us was Chên Ti-êrh's superior (see Chapter VI, n. 18). In *T'ang-shu*, ch. 2, he is simply termed Li-shan-fei. The *CYCCC* account gives no mention of Li Shih-min.

46. 十三年爲太原留守: "[Ta-yeh] 13th year [617], he became T'ai-yüan *liu-shou*." *Chiu T'ang-shu*, ch. 1, pp. 2a–2b; *T'ang-shu*, ch. 1, p. 2a; and *CYCCC*, ch. 1, p. 2a. In *TCTC*, ch. 183, p. 7a, this appointment precedes the defeat of Chên Ti-êrh (as in *T'ang-shu*, ch. 1, and in *CYCCC*, ch. 1) and hence in the *TCTC* is put in Ta-yeh 12th year (616).

47. In working out this chronology, I have followed the *Sui-shu* for the day of the battle and the *Chiu T'ang-shu* and the *CYCCC* for the date of Li Yüan's becoming *liu-shou*, since, as far as I know, they are the oldest and most reliable sources.

from the northern part of the country,[48] so that any commission from the Emperor could only be a confirmation of power already largely in the hands of Li Yüan. If the appointment was regularly made, and there is a possibility that it was not,[49] it was a mark of recognition and trust from the legitimate government of the empire. The Duke of T'ang seems to have accepted it as such and to have continued to be loyal to Emperor Yang until other circumstances constrained him to change his course.

Before turning to the specific problem of the situation in T'ai-yüan, however, let us note what was Li Yüan's position in relation to the whole empire.

In concluding this outline of political conditions in China at the beginning of the year 617, it is apparent that the Duke of T'ang was in an especially advantageous position. Related to the imperial house, of a distinguished official family and with a personal record of faithful service to the Sui dynasty, he was one to whom the upper classes and those still loyal to the Sui might look for leadership in a time of trouble. To the people, the name Li, fulfilling the popular ballad, would seem prophetic. And to all classes the prestige of recent military successes against foes within and without the region of Shansi must have had its effect.

This territory itself was perhaps the most significant factor in giving the Duke of T'ang a more favorable position in 617 than those held by others, who were soon to become his rivals for control of the empire. In the more populous north China plain, rebel hordes and loyal troops played a game of shifting political power with little in the way of natural defenses to assure stability in any given territory. From that area Shansi is cut off by the ranges of the T'ai-hang and Wu-t'ai Mountains.[50] Within these natural barriers the ruler of the Fên River valley might organize and establish his power without great risk of being overwhelmed in the civil wars of the rest of the country. We have had an example of this fact in recent Chinese history when almost

48. *Chiu T'ang-shu*, ch. 1, p. 2b.
49. Note the use of 爲 in the text of the *Chiu T'ang-shu* quoted above, n. 46.
50. 五臺山.

continuously from the establishment of the Republic until the invasion of the Japanese, Yen Hsi-shan maintained his authority in Shansi in spite of disturbed and changing conditions in other provinces. Similarly, in 616–617, the Duke of T'ang was fortunate to gain control in that region.

Several other factors in Li Yüan's rise to power, discussed in the following chapters, contributed materially to his success. Without the ability and enterprise of his son Li Shih-min, without other skillful advisors, and without Turkish coöperation, he might not have attained preëminence in the empire. Nevertheless, it is well to keep in mind what we have shown to be the initial advantages enjoyed by the Duke of T'ang at the time of his taking control of T'ai-yüan.

IX. BEGINNINGS OF REVOLT IN T'AI-YÜAN

LIU WÊN-CHING PLOTS WITH LI SHIH-MIN

Conditions in the commandery of T'ai-yüan at the commencement of 617 illustrated in intensified form the general disturbed state of the country. Swarms of people from the surrounding area had fled from the menace of bandits and had found refuge within the city walls until at this time several tens of thousands of persons were to be found there.[1] With the Duke of T'ang at their head and with the numbers of "brave gentlemen" (*hao-chieh*) who had gathered at his headquarters this body of people may be said to have constituted a potential force of some significance. It was important for all concerned whether they should remain loyal to the Sui or should take separate action leading to independent political power. The fact that within six months a revolution had successfully been accomplished, whereby those loyal to Emperor Yang had been disposed of and the Duke of T'ang had reached a position of undisputed authority in T'ai-yüan, leads us to surmise that he had a strong party of followers who were working consistently for his advancement.

Little is recorded concerning any such party or its leaders. Li Yüan's own share in the responsibility for the enterprise is stressed in the *Court Journal* of Wên Ta-ya.[2] The latter was official recorder at the Duke of T'ang's headquarters during most, if not all, of the year. In his account[3] he describes Li Yüan as the

1. *T'ang-shu*, ch. 2, p. 2a. It seems probable that the city of Chin-yang (Chin-yang-hsien 晉陽縣) to the west of the Fên River is implied. This was the seat of government of T'ai-yüan-chün (the commandery) and the location of Chin-yang Palace (see below, n. 10). The district, T'ai-yüan-hsien, at that time was to the northeast across the river.

2. 溫大雅, (b. before 574, d. 626–637). *CCBN*, p. 1290. Biography in *Chiu T'ang-shu*, ch. 61 (Tr. W. Bingham, "Wên Ta-ya: The First Recorder of T'ang History," *Journal of the American Oriental Society*, Vol. 57, No. 4 (December, 1937), pp. 368–374.

3. *CYCCC*, ch. 1.

principal and real leader. On the other hand the authors of the standard T'ang histories give to his son, Li Shih-min, and to the latter's friends the credit for taking the offensive in the revolt. They have included many details concerning Li Shih-min which are not even mentioned by Wên Ta-ya.

Their narratives, being the official ones, are best suited as a starting point for investigation. Hence the story here given is presented, not as a final analysis of the subject, but as a preliminary outline to show what are the standard accounts of the dynastic histories.

In the standard histories we learn that the Duke of T'ang was slow to take advantage of the favorable position in which he found himself in T'ai-yüan. There were others, however, at Chin-yang, where Li Yüan had his headquarters, who realized the opportunities for personal advancement and power in a region crowded with people, cut off from the central authorities, and now governed by a successful general bearing the auspicious name of Li. The local official in charge of the city of Chin-yang was an ambitious schemer named Liu Wên-ching.[4] "Believing that Kao-tsu was a man of world ambition he closely allied himself to him and trusted him."[5] Liu Wên-ching became one of the prime movers behind Li Yüan's rebellion.

At the time when he gained complete control in T'ai-yüan the Duke of T'ang was accompanied by his second son, Li Shih-min, who had recently aided him in his operations against bandits. Li Yüan was a faithful and able officer of the Sui, yet he is described as cautious and slow in comparison with Li Shih-min.[6] The son realized the opportunity for independent action and was secretly planning revolution. He was on the look-out for just such men as Liu Wên-ching.

4. 劉文靜, 568–619. *CCBN*, p. 1435. Biography in *Chiu T'ang-shu*, ch. 57, and in *T'ang-shu*, ch. 88 (Tr. Pfizmaier, "Gründung des Thang," pp. 71–78).

5. *Chiu T'ang-shu*, ch. 57, p. 6a. Cf. *T'ang-shu*, ch. 88, p. 1a.

6. Such is the general impression gained from the dynastic histories and the *TCTC*. The *CYCCC*, on the other hand, indicates that Li Shih-min at this time was simply following his father's instructions (ch. 1, p. 3b). See also n. 42.

On every occasion he humbled himself in association with the gentry and spared no expense in providing for the maintenance of strangers who came to him. Hence the whole crowd of robbers as well as the really influential men [lit. the heroes, those aiding others with influence and strength] were all willing to serve him to the death.[7]

Here was the man with whom Liu Wên-ching might work. After studiously observing Li Shih-min he spoke to his friend P'ei Chi,[8] Associate Supervisor[9] of the imperial palace at Chin-yang,[10] saying:

He [Li Shih-min] is an unusual man. In "broadmindedness"[11] he is in a class with Kao-tsu of the Han dynasty,[12] and in military spirit like T'ai-tsu of the Wei dynasty.[13] Although he is young, he is talented.[14]

Hence it was natural that Li Shih-min and Liu Wên-ching soon became close friends. From their intimacy developed plans which were to have important consequences in the history of China.

Some time after Li Shih-min came to T'ai-yüan, Liu Wên-ching

7. *Chiu T'ang-shu*, ch. 2, p. 2a. Cf. *T'ang-shu*, ch. 2, p. 1b.
8. 裴寂, 560-619. *CCBN*, p. 1382. Biography in *Chiu T'ang-shu*, ch. 57, and in *T'ang-shu*, ch. 88 (Tr. Pfizmaier, "Gründung des Thang," pp. 78-86).
9. *Fu-chien* 副監.
10. Chin-yang kung, 晉陽宮.
11. 大度.
12. 漢高祖, personal name Liu Chi 劉季, 247-195 B.C. First Emperor of the Han Dynasty. *GBD* 1334. *CCBN*, p. 1359. Biography in Ssŭ-ma Ch'ien, *Shih-chi*, ch. 8 (Tr. Edouard Chavannes, *Les Mémoires historiques de Se-ma Ts'ien* [Paris, 1895-1905], ch. 8), and in *Han-shu* 漢書, standard history of the Former Han dynasty, by Pan Ku 班固 (A.D. 32-92) and Pan Chao 班昭 (d. A.D. 114-120), chs. 1A-1B (Tr. Homer H. Dubs, *The History of the Former Han Dynasty by Pan Ku* Vol. I [Baltimore, 1938], ch. 1).
13. 魏太祖, personal name Ts'ao Ts'ao 曹操, A.D. 155-220. Founder of the Wei dynasty of the Three Kingdoms period. *GBD* 2013. *CCBN*, p. 993. Biographical material in *San-kuo-chih* 三國志, standard history of the Three Kingdoms, by Ch'ên Shou 陳壽 [A.D. 233-297. *GBD* 245], ch. 1.
14. *Chiu T'ang-shu*, ch. 57, p. 6a. Cf. *T'ang-shu*, ch. 88, p. 1b, ff. for all passages referring to Liu Wên-ching.

was incriminated on account of a marriage connection with the rebel Li Mi and, by the Emperor's order, detained in prison. In spite of the dangerous implication which might result, Li Shih-min visited Liu Wên-ching in gaol and they there plotted together against the government.[15]

Li Shih-min asked him for advice in the matter of drawing up some plan of action and the following was Liu Wên-ching's answer:

"Now Li Mi has for a long while been besieging Lo-i [i.e. Lo-yang]. The Emperor is a fugitive 'South of the Huai [River].'[16] Great rebels, who get influence over more than one prefecture [chou] or commandery [chün], and petty bandits, who have their lairs in mountains and swamps, are innumerable. It is only necessary for the true lord to drive the imperial chariot and seize control and he will certainly find favor with heaven and man . . .

"Now all the people of T'ai-yüan who have fled from the bandits and rebels have come into this city. I, Wên-ching, having been Magistrate for several years, know the 'brave gentlemen' of this district. At an instant summons to rally I could get a hundred thousand men. The troops under the direction of your Excellencies [i.e. the Duke of T'ang and his family] are a further force of several tens of thousands. Should you but say the word, who will dare not to follow? Take advantage of the lack [of preparedness] to enter the 'Region within the Passes'. Give the word of command to the empire and in less than half a year the founding of an imperial family may be accomplished."[17]

Li Shih-min smiled and said: "Your words agree exactly with my intention."[18]

[Together[19]] they then organized the strangers who had already been made welcome[20] and secretly planned to initiate the cause of "Righteous-

15. *Chiu T'ang-shu*, ch. 57, p. 6a, and *T'ang-shu*, ch. 2, p. 2a.
16. Huai-nan 淮南.
17. . . . 不盈半歲帝業可成. *Chiu T'ang-shu*, ch. 57, p. 6b. Cf. *T'ang-shu*, ch. 88, p. 1b, and *TCTC*, ch. 183, p. 18a.
18. *T'ang-shu*, ch. 88, p. 1b: 君言正與我意合. Cf. *TCTC*, ch. 183, p. 18a: 君言正合我意. The *Chiu T'ang-shu*, ch. 57, p. 6b, here gives: 君言正合人意.
19. Cf. *T'ang-shu*, ch. 2, p. 2a.
20. *Pin-k'o* 賓客.

ness".[21] They awaited conditions opportune for starting. As they feared that the Duke of T'ang would not agree to their plan, their thought and deliberations over ways and means of persuading him continued for a long time.[22]

As Garrison Commander of T'ai-yüan the Duke of T'ang was also responsible for the supervision of the Chin-yang Palace. P'ei Chi, as Associate Supervisor, was directly in charge.[23] The two were very good friends and often spent long nights and days feasting and gambling together. Knowing this, Liu Wên-ching wished to get P'ei Chi to broach the subject of their plans to the Duke of T'ang.[24]

Liu Wên-ching then brought about friendly relations between P'ei Chi and Li Shih-min. The latter arranged a game of chance in which another man lost a quantity of money to P'ei Chi, who was thus persuaded to become a party to their schemes.[25] Thence forward these three—Liu Wên-ching, P'ei Chi and Li Shih-min worked together to take advantage of events in Shansi and the empire as a whole to strengthen the Duke of T'ang's position and practically to force him to take up arms against the Sui.

INVASION, INTRIGUE, AND ARGUMENT

We have seen that in the preceding year, 616, Turks had invaded the north of Shansi and had been repulsed by the Duke of T'ang. The borders remained unsettled and in the winter of 616–617 pressure from that direction continued to affect the situation at T'ai-yüan. On several occasions the Turks broke through the frontiers and at least once raided the important

21. 義, the expression here used, should be compared with 義兵, used elsewhere in this connection. (Cf. below, p. 90, ff.) The latter, meaning "Righteous Troops" or "Soldiers of Justice", is a name which has often been used in China by those who, at different periods, have pretended to be taking up arms in the name of righteousness. See Chavannes, *Mémoires Historiques*, Vol. II, p. 376, n. 2.

22. *Chiu T'ang-shu*, ch. 57, p. 6b.

23. *T'ang-shu*, ch. 1, p. 2b.

24. *Chiu T'ang-shu*, ch. 57, pp. 1b and 6b.

25. *Chiu T'ang-shu*, ch. 57, pp. 6b and 1b.

border commandery, Ma-i-chün. In order again to assist the Commandery Administrator, Wang Jên-kung, the Duke of T'ang sent north his Associate General,²⁶ Kao Chün-ya,²⁷ with troops. These were united with those of Wang Jên-kung in opposing the Turks, but were defeated by them. When the news of this defeat reached Chiang-tu (an event which must have taken some time, considering the disturbed conditions of the country), Emperor Yang sent an envoy to seize the Duke of T'ang and bring him to Chiang-tu. The possibility of such imprisonment caused Li Yüan much fear and anxiety.²⁸

This seemed to Li Shih-min an opportune occasion. He thereupon had Liu Wên-ching and P'ei Chi go to the Duke of T'ang to urge him to adopt their plan for independent action. Their line of argument was as follows:

"... Now great rebellions have already broken out. Are you, occupying a position subject to suspicion and [on the other hand] undertaking meritorious work too great to be rewarded, planning to continue safe and sound? He whose subordinate generals are defeated in battle may be held responsible for their guilt. The affair is indeed urgent. It is absolutely necessary to make a plan.

"The soldiers and horses of the region of Chin-yang are trained and strong. The store-houses within the Palace Inspectorate are filled with abundance. Taking advantage of this to start things one can achieve great merit.

"In the Region within the Passes at the imperial court the Prince of Tai²⁹ is an immature minor. Influential and notable men are all revolting, but there is not yet any real leader whom the people will follow.³⁰

26. *Fu-chiang* 副將.
27. 高君雅, d. 617. He also had the honorary military title *hu-ya lang-chiang* 虎牙郎將 and, instead of "Associate General", he is also designated "Associate Garrison Commander", *fu-liu-shou* 副留守. *T'ang-shu*, ch. 1, p. 4a.
28. *T'ang-shu*, ch. 1, p. 2b; *Chiu T'ang-shu*, ch. 57, p. 6b; *TCTC*, ch. 183, p. 18b.
29. 代王, personal name Yang Yu 楊侑, later known as Kung-ti 恭帝, 605–619. *CCBN*, pp. 1213–1214. Early life and "reign" in *Sui-shu*, ch. 5, and in *Pei-shih*, ch. 12.
30. *TCTC*, ch. 183, p. 19a, gives "they do not yet know to whom to adhere" 未知所附.

"We desire that you should raise troops and proceed westward into the Region within the Passes in order to follow out the great [imperial] undertaking. Why should you be imprisoned by a lone envoy?"[31]

The Duke of T'ang assented to their plan. During this time Li Shih-min made secret and solemn alliance with desperate members of the military class and deliberated with Liu Wên-ching and others. They discussed a date for raising troops.[32]

Meanwhile Emperor Yang again sent an envoy to the north, this time with a pardon for Li Yüan, who forthwith took no active part in preparations that others might make for rebellion.[33] Although the Emperor might pardon yet he could no longer control officials in such a distant region as T'ai-yüan, nor could he prevent Li Yüan's son and friends from taking things into their own hands.

When Li Shih-min saw that his father, although acquiescing in the idea, did nothing himself toward acting independently, he

... commanded [Liu] Wên-ching to forge an imperial order[34] of Emperor Yang announcing that [in] T'ai-yüan, Hsi-ho, Yen-mên, and Ma-i [commanderies in central and north Shansi] men between the ages of twenty and fifty were all to enroll as soldiers and at an appointed date at the end of the year were to assemble at Cho-chün to attack "East of the Liao".

This seems to have increased the general discontent in that region.[35]

At this time, as we have seen, Li Shih-min had won P'ei Chi to his cause and was getting him to influence Li Yüan. P'ei Chi thereupon selected from the imperial palace at Chin-yang a girl (or girls) whom he handed over to the Duke of T'ang for his pleasure.[36] The two men continued to feast and drink together. Liu Wên-ching, knowing this, urged P'ei Chi to arouse Li Yüan, but P'ei Chi's repeated urging had no effect.[37]

31. *Chiu T'ang-shu*, ch. 57, p. 7a. Cf. *T'ang-shu*, ch. 88, p. 2a.
32. *Chiu T'ang-shu*, ch. 57, p. 7a.
33. *Chiu T'ang-shu*, ch. 57, p. 7a; and *T'ang-shu*, ch. 1, pp. 2b–3a.
34. *Ch'ih* 勅.
35. *Chiu T'ang-shu*, ch. 57, p. 7a.
36. *Chiu T'ang-shu*, ch. 57, p. 1b; and *T'ang-shu*, ch. 1, p. 2b.
37. *Chiu T'ang-shu*, ch. 57, p. 7a.

Finally, on one occasion when Li Yüan was tipsy with wine, P'ei Chi made a clear statement, saying:

"Your second son [i.e. Li Shih-min] secretly keeps troops and horses with the idea of raising a 'Standard of Righteousness'. This is precisely because of my having presented you with a palace girl. It is feared that the affair may be exposed and may go as far as punishment by execution. The urgency [i.e. Li Shih-min's action] is just because of this.[38]

"Now the empire is seriously disturbed. Outside the city gates all are robbers and bandits. If you keep to a narrow interpretation of your duties,[39] death and irretrievable loss may come in one day. But if you raise a 'Righteous Army', you certainly will obtain the imperial throne. The crowd's feelings are already in agreement with this. What is your intention?"[40]

At this point Li Shih-min also entered the room and explained his actions. At first Li Yüan made a pretence of not allowing it and wanted to seize his son to send him to the officials. Finally he gave his consent, saying, "I love you. How can I bear to report you?"[41] And to P'ei Chi he said, "If truly my boy has this plan and everything is already decided, I may as well follow it."[42]

38. *Chiu T'ang-shu*, ch. 57, p. 2a. Cf. *TCTC*, ch. 183, p. 19a. The punishment, *chu* 誅, generally implies execution, but not necessarily so.
39. 守小節.
40. *Chiu T'ang-shu*, ch. 57, pp. 1b–2a. Cf. *T'ang-shu*, ch. 1, p. 2b, and ch. 88, p. 4b.
41. *T'ang-shu*, ch. 1, p. 2b.
42. *Chiu T'ang-shu*, ch. 57, p. 2a. Cf. *ibid.*, ch. 57, p. 7b. I have inserted the whole incident of the Duke of T'ang's talk with P'ei Chi and Li Shih-min at this point because, while the different texts vary in their sequences of events, this incident thus coincides best with the order of events in the *Chiu T'ang-shu* biography of Liu Wên-ching, ch. 57, which seems to me to be the most logical of the accounts. My narrative also coincides with the few details given in the biography of Li Shih-min in *T'ang-shu*, ch. 2, p. 2a. His other biography, *Chiu T'ang-shu*, ch. 2, gives little indication of how these events occurred.

Mention must be made, however, of the fact that in *TCTC*, ch. 183, pp. 18a–20a, we have a version of these events in quite a different order and with many additional details, especially concerning Li Shih-min. One of the most interesting of these, a conversation between Li Shih-min and his father, including a reference to the prophecy concerning the Li

LIU WU-CHOU THREATENS T'AI-YÜAN

Even if Li Yüan hoped any longer to remain inactive, outside events soon made action imperative. Some of the numerous rebellions that occurred in the early part of 617 outside of Shansi have already been mentioned. The annals tell us that "hosts of rebels were rising up like bees".[43] These were mostly far removed from T'ai-yüan. But now a dangerous combination was formed directly to the north of this region.

At Ma-i, a local official sympathetic with the Turks, Liu Wu-chou,[44] had on March 20 rebelled against and killed his superior, the Commandery Administrator Wang Jên-kung. Then, as in the case of other rebels to the west in the Ordos, he turned north to ally himself with the Turkish Khan, Shih-pi, and later received from the latter the designation of Khan.[45]

It is significant at this point to note the strength and prestige of Shih-pi Khan, the ruler of those powerful nomads, the Eastern Turks, whose hostility contributed to the downfall of Emperor Yang and whose friendship or enmity played an important part during the first twelve years of the T'ang dynasty. He was then probably the post powerful ruler in northeast Asia.

> During the anarchy and political division at the end of the Sui innumerable Chinese took refuge with Shih pi. Thereupon his great strength and abundant power infringed on that of China . . .[46]

---

name and the execution of Li Chin-ts'ai (Li Hun), *TCTC*, ch. 183, pp. 18b–19a, has been fairly well translated in Fitzgerald, *Son of Heaven* . . . , pp. 33–34. (Mr. Fitzgerald's general account of the events of this time does not entirely accord with the facts, as far as I have been able to determine them.) In the *CYCCC*, ch. 1, account of this time, Li Shih-min's share in the events is noticeable by its absence.

43. *Chiu T'ang-shu*, ch. 1, p. 2b.
44. 劉武周, d. 622. *CCBN*, p. 1450. Biography in *Chiu T'ang-shu*, ch. 55, and in *T'ang-shu*, ch. 86 (Tr. Pfizmaier, "Gründung des Thang," pp. 29–34). Liu Wu-chou's title at this time was *hsiao-wei* 校尉. It is not clear what was the function of the holder of this office at the end of the Sui period.
45. *Sui-shu*, ch. 4, p. 13b; *Chiu T'ang-shu*, ch. 55, p. 9a; *T'ang-shu*, ch. 1, p. 3a, and ch. 86, pp. 7b–8a; *TCTC*, ch. 183, pp. 11a–11b.
46. *Sui-shu*, ch. 84, p. 15a. Cf. *T'ang-shu*, ch. 221A, p. 9a.

From the Khitan[47] and Shih-wei[48] in the east extending to include the T'u-yü-hun and Kao-ch'ang in the west all the states were his subjects or dependencies. His archers were over a million. There had never before been such prosperity among the northern barbarians.[49]

Such men as Hsieh Chü, Tou Chien-tê, Wang Shih-ch'ung, Liu Wu-chou, Liang Shih-tu, Li Kuei,[50] and Kao K'ai-tao, although usurping exalted titles [such as the title of prince or emperor], all "faced the north", declared themselves his vassals and accepted his entitling them Khan. Their envoys going back and forth were always within view of each other on the road.[51]

Liu Wu-chou had, with the aid of these Turks, moved south from Ma-i in the spring of 617.[52] He had taken Sang-kan-chên[53] (northeast of Ma-i), Yen-mên, and Lou-fan (modern Ching-lo) and was now, in about the latter half of May or beginning of June,[54] at the upper Fên valley in possession of the Fên-yang Palace. With horses from the Turks he consolidated his position by seizing Ting-hsiang,[55] northwest of Ma-i. It was at this time that he was invested by the Turks with the title of Ting-yang

47. 契丹 (Ch'i-tan), tribes who inhabited the region of present northern Jehol. For their history see *Sui-shu*, ch. 84 (Tr. Pfizmaier, "Fremdländischen Reiche," pp. 478-480); *Pei-shih*, ch. 94; *Chiu T'ang-shu*, ch. 199B; *T'ang-shu*, ch. 219.

48. 室韋, tribes in present northern Manchuria. For their history see *Sui-shu*, ch. 84 (Tr. Pfizmaier, *op. cit.*, pp. 480-483); *Pei-shih*, ch. 94; *Chiu T'ang-shu*, ch. 199B; *T'ang-shu*, ch. 219.

49. *Chiu T'ang-shu*, ch. 194A, p. 1a.

50. 李軌, d. 619. *CCBN*, p. 409. Biography in *Chiu T'ang-shu*, ch. 55, and in *T'ang-shu*, ch. 86 (Tr. Pfizmaier, "Gründung des Thang," pp. 22-28).

51. *Sui-shu*, ch. 84, pp. 15a-15b. Cf. *T'ang-shu*, ch. 215A, p. 6a. Some of these mentioned as turning to Shih-pi did so after the middle of Ta-yeh 13th year (617).

52. Ta-yeh 13th year, 2nd and 3rd moons (March 13–May 10, 617).

53. 桑乾鎮. *Sui-shu*, ch. 4, p. 13b. See Appendix D: Ta-yeh 13th year (617), 2nd moon, day 39.

54. 4th moon (May 11–June 8).

55. 定襄郡.

Khan[56] and proclaimed himself Emperor and his wife Empress.[57] A strong combination thus threatened Li Yüan's position from the north.

This was the critical moment in the fortunes of the Duke of T'ang. Discussion arose as to the correct mode of procedure, since some of the officials remained loyal to Emperor Yang and did not wish to act without his orders. Li Yüan, however, assembled his "generals and civil officials" and addressed them:

"I am now Garrison Commander and yet bandits occupy the detached palace [i.e. the Fên-yang Palace]. To let the bandits continue their ravages without their meeting due punishment is a crime worthy of death. Yet in sending out troops one ought to wait for an authorization.[58] Now Chiang-tu is cut off and far away. Under the circumstances what course should I pursue?"

The generals and civil officials all said: "The one who alone can be responsible for the fortunes of the nation is Your Excellency."[59]

The Duke of T'ang approved and ordered Li Shih-min, Liu Wên-ching and their followers to enlist troops. These, as we have seen, had already gained a large secret following. Within ten days Li Yüan had under his command a host of about ten thousand. In this matter Li Yüan seems to have employed Li Shih-min and his friends in place of his regular assistants.[60]

In the biography of Liu Wên-ching we learn more about Li Shih-min's share in these preparations, whether with or without his father's approval. Hearing of Liu Wu-chou's advance,

... Li Shih-min sent out Liu Wên-ching together with Ch'ang-sun Shun-tê[61] and others, each with a specific assignment, to enlist troops with the avowed intention of punishing Liu Wu-chou.[62] Also he ordered

56. 定楊可汗.
57. *Chiu T'ang-shu*, ch. 1, p. 2b; ch. 55, pp. 9a–9b; ch. 57, p. 7b; *T'ang-shu*, ch. 1, p. 3b; and ch. 86, p. 8a. Cf. *TCTC*, ch. 183, p. 14a.
58. *Pao* 報.
59. *T'ang-shu*, ch. 1, p. 3b.
60. *Chiu T'ang-shu*, ch. 1, p. 2b; *T'ang-shu*, ch. 1, pp. 3b–4a.
61. 長孫順德, d. in reign of T'ai-tsung (627–649). *GBD* 141. *CCBN*, p. 614. Biography in *Chiu T'ang-shu*, ch. 58, and in *T'ang-shu*, ch. 105.
62. 以討武周爲辭.

Liu Wên-ching and P'ei Chi to forge an imperial order[63] for the issuance of goods from the storehouse of the Palace Inspectorate to provide the supplies for the use of the Garrison Commander. And so they had enlisted troops and assembled a host.[64]

The raising of this army aroused the suspicions of Li Yüan's subordinates, the Associate Generals[65] or Associate Garrison Commanders,[66] Wang Wei[67] and Kao Chün-ya, who therefore plotted against his life. But a counterplot engineered by Li Shih-min and Liu Wên-ching succeeded and the two assistants were seized on the charge of planning a revolt. This took place on the first day of a new cycle (June 23, 617).[68] A Turk raid happened two days later, Kao Chün-ya and Wang Wei were accused of having called them in, and, with that as an excuse, were duly decapitated.[69]

The die was cast. The Duke of T'ang had now definitely broken with the Sui authorities. Li Shih-min and his friends' plotting and planning had accomplished the result they desired. It could only be a matter of days before Li Yüan declared openly that his increased military forces were not raised simply to oppose Liu Wu-chou, but that they were "Righteous Troops"[70] in open rebellion against the Emperor.

63. *Fu-ch'ih* 符勅.
64. *Chiu T'ang-shu*, ch. 57, p. 7b. Cf. *T'ang-shu*, ch. 88, p. 2b, which gives the last part as follows: . . . 佐軍興.
65. *Chiu T'ang-shu*, ch. 1, p. 2b.
66. *T'ang-shu*, ch. 1, p. 4a.
67. 王威, d. 617. He was also Assistant Administrator of the Commandery (*chün-ch'êng*). *Chiu T'ang-shu*, ch. 1, p. 2b.
68. Ta-yeh 13th year, 5th moon, day 1.
69. Ta-yeh 13th year (617), 5th moon, day 3. *Chiu T'ang-shu*, ch. 1, p. 2b; *T'ang-shu*, ch. 1, p. 4a; and *Sui-shu*, ch. 4, p. 14a. Further details in *Chiu T'ang-shu*, ch. 57, pp. 7b-8a; *T'ang-shu*, ch. 88, p. 2b; *CYCCC*, ch. 1, pp. 5b-6a; and *TCTC*, ch. 183, pp. 21a-21b. The *CYCCC* account makes it seem possible that the Turk raid was arranged from within T'ai-yüan to aid Li Yüan in getting rid of those hostile to his plans.
70. 義兵. *Chiu T'ang-shu*, ch. 1, p. 2b; *T'ang-shu*, ch. 1, p. 4a. *Sui-shu*, ch. 4, p. 14a, gives 義師.

X. CAMPAIGN OF THE "RIGHTEOUS ARMY"

INDEPENDENT ACTION

A time of waiting now gave way to one of positive independent action. By diplomatic, administrative and military means, events were started which eventually culminated in the establishment of one of China's most famous dynasties.

Strengthened by his new force of loyal troops, provisioned from the imperial stores, and no longer dependent on orders from Chiang-tu, the Duke of T'ang was in a position to resist a body of Turks on their last raid, even though they came with a force of several thousand.[1] He now desired to enter into active alliance with them, for if he were to leave T'ai-yüan he must make sure that his rear would not be attacked. Although it does not appear that he negotiated with Liu Wu-chou, it seems probable that the latter did not dare to move south as long as Shih-pi Khan to his north was friendly with Li Yüan. Furthermore, the Duke of T'ang must also obtain horses from the Turks if he were to contend successfully against the imperial troops. Hence he sent Liu Wên-ching as an envoy to Shih-pi Khan and invited the latter to coöperate by leading troops in the campaign.[2]

The Turks also were interested in estimating the situation in T'ai-yüan. A Turk named K'ang Shao-li,[3] who may have been a close relative of the Khan, arrived during the next month with a thousand head of horses for trade and was present just before Li Yüan commenced his march on Ch'ang-an.[4] Thus Shih-pi

1. See references, Chapter IX, n. 69.
2. Ta-yeh 13th year, 5th moon, day 11 (July 3, 617). *Chiu T'ang-shu*, ch. 1, pp. 2b–3a; ch. 57, p. 8a; *T'ang-shu*, ch. 1, p. 4a; and ch. 88, p. 2b. *CYCCC*, ch. 1, pp. 6b–7b gives details differing somewhat from those in the dynastic histories.
3. 康稍利; he was a *tegin* (*t'ê-chin*), a title used for a son or younger brother of the Khan; *Chiu T'ang-shu*, ch. 194A, p. 1b.
4. *CYCCC*, ch. 1, p. 8b and pp. 10b–11a. *TCTC*, ch. 184, pp. 2a–3b.

Khan might be well informed as to the importance of the Duke of T'ang's rebellion and its possibilities of success.

At about the same time that the Duke of T'ang ordered the raising of troops to combat Liu Wu-chou, he secretly sent an envoy to summon his eldest son and heir,[5] Li Chien-ch'êng,[6] and his fourth son, Li Yüan-chi,[7] who were then in Ho-tung.[8]   They arrived in T'ai-yüan a few days after Liu Wên-ching had left for the north and on that same day the Duke of T'ang issued his proclamation to the whole land, whereby he announced to all the commanderies the raising of "Righteous Troops".[9]

START OF THE CAMPAIGN

The rest of that month was spent in organizing and preparing for the campaign which would take them to the western capital. What may be called a "Generalissimo's Headquarters" was established with the Duke of T'ang as chief.   Beneath him were six armies[10] divided into two groups: "the Three Armies of the Left" and "the Three Armies of the Right".   These were assigned to Li Chien-ch'êng and Li Shih-min respectively.   The organization as it was then set up can best be understood by direct quotation from the annals of the dynastic histories.

6th moon, . . . day 30 [July 22, 617], the Duke of T'ang established a Generalissimo's Headquarters and set up the Three Armies, dividing them into Left and Right.   He appointed: his eldest son Li Chien-

---

5. *Shih-tzŭ* 世子.
6. 李建成, 589-626. *CCBN*, p. 404. Biography in *Chiu T'ang-shu*, ch. 64, and in *T'ang-shu*, ch. 79.
7. 李元吉, 603-626. *CCBN*, p. 375. Biography in same *chüan* as Li Chien-ch'êng.
8. *Chiu T'ang-shu*, ch. 1, p. 2b.
9. Ta-yeh 13th year, 6th moon?, day 16 ([July 8?], 617). *CYCCC*, ch. 1, p. 8a; *TCTC*, ch. 184, p. 1a-1b; *T'ang-shu*, ch. 1, p. 4a. According to P. Hoang, *Concordance des Chronologies*, p. 184, "day 16" (*chi-mao*) is the 30th day of the 5th moon and "6th moon, day 16" is an impossible date.
10. *Chün* 軍.

ch'êng to be Duke of Lung-hsi,[11] Commander-in-Chief of the Left,[12] all the Armies of the Left being under his control; Li Shih-min to be Duke of Tun-huang,[13] Commander-in-Chief of the Right,[14] all the Armies of the Right being under his control; P'ei Chi to be Chief of Staff[15] of the Generalissimo's Headquarters; Liu Wên-ching to be *ssŭ-ma*;[16] Yin K'ai-shan [Yin Chiao],[17] the District Magistrate of Shih-ai,[18] to be Clerk;[19] Liu Chêng-hui[20] to be *shu*;[21] Ch'ang-sun Shun-tê, Liu Hung-chi,[22] Tou Tsung,[23] and others were divided between the Left and Right Armies.[24]

Another important member of this group, Wên Ta-ya, was appointed Staff Officer in charge of Records.[25]

It has already been mentioned that Li Shih-min obtained provisions from the imperial stores. Now that he and his father were in open conflict with the Sui forces, they used these stores for public benefit as well as their own. "They opened granaries

11. 隴西公.
12. *Tso-ling ta-tu-tu* 左領大都督 (lit. Great *tu-tu* in Command of the Left).
13. 燉煌公.
14. *Yu-ling ta-tu-tu* 右領大都督.
15. *Chang-shih* 長史.
16. *Ssŭ-ma* 司馬. This is an ancient title, but the actual function at this period has not been determined.
17. 殷嶠, *tzŭ* K'ai-shan 開山, d. ca. 622. *CCBN*, p. 814. Biography in *Chiu T'ang-shu*, ch. 58, and in *T'ang-shu*, ch. 90.
18. 石艾縣長.
19. *Yüan* 掾.
20. 劉政會, d. 635. *CCBN*, p. 1449. Biography in *Chiu T'ang-shu*, ch. 58, and in *T'ang-shu*, ch. 90.
21. *Shu* 屬.
22. 劉弘基, 582-650. *CCBN*, p. 1437. Biography in *Chiu T'ang-shu*, ch. 58, and in *T'ang-shu*, ch. 90.
23. 竇琮. *CCBN*, p. 1773. Biography in *Chiu T'ang-shu*, ch. 61, and in *T'ang-shu*, ch. 95.
24. *Chiu T'ang-shu*, ch. 1, p. 3a. Cf. *T'ang-shu*, ch. 1, pp. 4a-4b, and *TCTC*, ch. 184, pp. 2a-2b. According to the *T'ang-shu*, these appointments were made two weeks earlier at the same time as the proclamation of the "Righteous Army". But the *TCTC* agrees with the *Chiu T'ang-shu* in giving 6th moon, day 30.
25. *Chi-shih tsan-chün* 記室參軍. *Chiu T'ang-shu*, ch. 61, p. 1b, and *TCTC*, ch. 184, pp. 2a-2b.

and storehouses to relieve the destitute. Far and near rever-
berated with the good news and rallied to them.''[26]

Meanwhile they were losing no time in getting started with
the campaign—the march on Ch'ang-an. Five days after his
public proclamation, the Duke of T'ang had sent Li Shih-min
with an advance guard some sixty miles down the Fên River
valley. The son accomplished his mission by taking Hsi-ho-chün,
the next commandery downstream.[27]

Li Yüan himself was getting the main force in order. On
August 10 and 11[28] he led forth out of T'ai-yüan a body of thirty
thousand troops. Accompanied by the Western Turk Ta-nai[29]
and his host, they at once took the road down the Fên in the
direction of the Region within the Passes.[30] Thus the plans of
Li Shih-min, Liu Wên-ching and the rest were actually being put
into execution. The Duke of T'ang was on his way to conquer
Ch'ang-an.

He was not leaving T'ai-yüan undefended, however. His son
Li Yüan-chi did not accompany the expedition, but was com-
missioned to remain as General in Command of the Northern
Defences[31] and Garrison Commander of T'ai-yüan.[32]

The Duke of T'ang was not long in meeting with serious difficulties. Before reaching Ho-i[33] (present Ho-hsien) he found that
Sui forces under General Sung Lao-shêng[34] held a narrow defile
and thereby completely obstructed passage down the valley. At
this time a heavy rain commenced and lasted for over three
weeks. This literally put a damper on the spirits of the Righteous

26. *Chiu T'ang-shu*, ch. 1, p. 3a. Cf. *T'ang-shu*, ch. 1, p. 4b.
27. 6th moon, day 30 (July 22, 617). *Chiu T'ang-shu*, ch. 1, p. 3a,
and ch. 2, p. 2a; *T'ang-shu*, ch. 2, p. 2a. Further details in *CYCCC*,
ch. 1, pp. 9b–10a.
28. 7th moon, day 49 and day 50.
29. *TCTC*, ch. 184, p. 3b. See above, p. 34.
30. *Chiu T'ang-shu*, ch. 1, p. 3a; *T'ang-shu*, ch. 1, p. 4b; *CYCCC*,
ch. 2, p. 1; *TCTC*, ch. 184, p. 3b.
31. *Chên-pei chiang-chün* 鎮北將軍.
32. *Chiu T'ang-shu*, ch. 1, p. 3a; *T'ang-shu*, ch. 1, p. 4b.
33. Ho-i (or Huo-i) 霍邑.
34. 宋老生.

Army. Provisions ran low and Li Yüan seriously considered returning to T'ai-yüan. Li Shih-min, however, persuaded his father to persist in his campaign.[35] Consequently, the Duke of T'ang then placed squarely on the shoulders of Li Shih-min the responsibility for the success or failure of their venture.[36]

MILITARY AND DIPLOMATIC SUCCESS

When the rain had stopped,[37] the Duke of T'ang two days later defeated Sung Lao-shêng and was able to push on down the valley of the Fên. Two weeks later he reached Lung-mên at the mouth of the Fên and was well along the way to Ch'ang-an.[38] Nearby in Ho-tung, however, Ch'ü-t'u T'ung,[39] a veteran general of the Sui, opposed Li Yüan. He took measures to prevent sympathizers from joining or aiding the T'ang army. His forces interrupted ferries and destroyed bridges.[40]

With the help of allies and by careful foresight, Li Yüan was able to proceed. On his arrival at Lung-mên he met the Eastern Turk leader, K'ang Shao-li, bringing to his aid a force of five hundred soldiers and two thousand head of horses. With them was Li Yüan's envoy, Liu Wên-ching, who had successfully arranged an alliance with Shih-pi Khan.[41]

35. *Chiu T'ang-shu*, ch. 1, pp. 3a–3b; *T'ang-shu*, ch. 1, p. 4a. See also *CYCCC*, ch. 2, pp. 4b, ff.

36. *T'ang-shu*, ch. 2, p. 2a: ... 高祖窘曰起事者汝也. 成敗惟汝. Cf. *TCTC*, ch. 184, p. 5b.

37. Ta-yeh 13th year, 8th moon, day 16 (September 6, 617). *Chiu T'ang-shu*, ch. 2, p. 2b.

38. 8th moon, day 30 (September 20, 617). *Chiu T'ang-shu*, ch. 1, p. 3b; ch. 2, p. 2b; *T'ang-shu*, ch. 1, p. 4b; ch. 2, p. 2b.

39. 屈突通, 557–628. *CCBN*, p. 563. Biography in *Chiu T'ang-shu*, ch. 59, and in *T'ang-shu*, ch. 89 (Tr. Pfizmaier, "Seltsamkeiten aus den Zeiten der Thang," *Sitzungsber, d. k. Ak. d. Wiss. Phil.-hist. Classe*, Vol. XCIV [Vienna, 1879], pp. 11–18.)

40. *Chiu T'ang-shu*, ch. 1, p. 3b; *T'ang-shu*, ch. 1, p. 4b.

41. *Chiu T'ang-shu*, ch. 1, p. 3b; *T'ang-shu*, ch. 215A, p. 6a, and *TCTC*, ch. 184, p. 8a, give the above figures. But *Chiu T'ang-shu*, ch. 194A, p. 1b, and ch. 57, p. 8b, state that Shih-pi Khan sent K'ang Shao-li with a command of two thousand cavalry and a gift of a thousand horses. *T'ang-shu*, ch. 1, p. 4b, gives no figures.

In the negotiations with Shih-pi Khan, Liu Wên-ching had presented a plan which appealed to the Khan.

["Li Yüan and his party," he said] "desire to enter the capital together with the Khan's soldiers and horses. Population and land would go to the Duke of T'ang. Money and valuables [lit. money and silk, gold and jewels] would go to the Turks." Shih-pi [Khan] was greatly pleased....[42]

These reinforcements were the result.

The Turks were not his only allies. People who inhabited this region of Ho-tung, where Li Yüan had formerly successfully opposed banditry, volunteered their services and brought boats and carts to assist in the crossing of the Yellow River. Influential men from beyond that stream, including a bandit leader of P'ing-i-chün came with similar aid.[43]

CROSSING THE YELLOW RIVER

Even with this help it was a question as to how they should proceed. P'ei Chi advised subduing Ho-tung before they crossed the river into the Region within the Passes. Li Shih-min, on the other hand, wished his father to take advantage of the present friendliness of the people in that region and to act quickly in proceeding against Ch'ang-an.[44]

He requested that they advance the army within the passes, take Yung-fêng Granary [located near the strategic T'ung-kuan] in order to

42. *Chiu T'ang-shu*, ch. 57, p. 8b.   Cf. *T'ang-shu*, ch. 88, p. 3a; and *TCTC*, ch. 184, p. 4a.   A further note concerning Li Yüan's calling on the Turks for aid is contained in Sun Fu 孫甫, *T'ang-shih lun-tuan* 唐史論斷. (Eleventh century. Vol. LXXVII in *Hsüeh-chin t'ao-yüan* 學津討原, compiled by Chang Hai-p'êng 張海鵬, 1805. Photolithographic reprint, Commercial Press, Shanghai.)

43. *Chiu T'ang-shu*, ch. 1, p. 3b, and ch. 2, p. 2b; *T'ang-shu*, ch. 1, p. 4b.   For the first mention of Sun Hua 孫華, the bandit leader of P'ing-i, see above p. 70.   He arrived on 8th moon, day 39 (September 29, 617), according to *T'ang-shu*, ch. 1, p. 4b, and *CYCCC*, ch. 2, p. 11a. Calculation from the lunar calendar proves their correctness, although *Chiu T'ang-shu*, ch. 1, p. 3a, gives "9th moon, day 39," an impossible date. *TCTC*, ch. 184, p. 10b, leaves one in doubt.

44. *Chiu T'ang-shu*, ch. 57, pp. 2a-2b; *T'ang-shu*, ch. 88, p. 5a; and *Chiu T'ang-shu*, ch. 2, p. 3a.

relieve the poor and needy, and gather in the crowds of bandits with the purpose of [taking] the capital.[45]

The Duke of T'ang adopted a compromise by which he followed both plans. A division of forces was made; some remained to invest the commandery city of Ho-tung, while the rest of the army proceeded to cross the river in sections.

The crossing was still being effected when Ch'ü-t'u T'ung sent a subordinate general, Sang Hsien-ho,[46] with a force of several thousand to make a surprise attack on one of the divisions.[47] This developed into what seems to the author to have been the crucial event of the campaign the battle of Yin-ma Spring.[48] Li Shih-min had already crossed the river with the vanguard, which probably consisted only of light cavalry. When the main T'ang armies commenced to cross, they were in a particularly dangerous situation. The Sui general Sang Hsien-ho attacked and was at first successful. At that point, the annals inform us: "Li Shih-min with several hundred 'roving cavalry'[49] surprised Sang Hsien-ho's rear. Sang Hsien-ho was routed and the morale of the Righteous Army was again restored."[50]

This is the only account among five the present writer has seen that mentions Li Shih-min's taking part in the battle. The probability is that this cavalry was under his command, but that he did not personally take part in the battle. The "roving cavalry" was that of the Western Turk Ta-nai, who, as mentioned above, had been with Li Yüan from the start of the campaign. He was with the T'ang forces when Sang Hsien-ho made his surprise attack.

At the moment when many of the troops had already fled and withdrawn, Ta-nai, at the head of several hundred cavalry, made a sortie

---

45. *Ching-shih* 京師. *Chiu T'ang-shu*, ch. 2, p. 3a.
46. 桑顯和. His title was *hu-ya lang-chiang.*
47. Ta-yeh 13th year, 9th moon, day 52 (October 12, 617). *TCTC*, ch. 184, p. 10b, and *CYCCC*, ch. 2, pp. 11a–11b, indicate this date.
48. Yin-ma-ch'uan 飲馬泉. Besides the accounts noted above, see also *Chiu T'ang-shu*, ch. 59, p. 2b; *T'ang-shu*, ch. 89, p. 2a.
49. 遊騎.
50. *Chiu T'ang-shu*, ch. 1, p. 4a. (Date not definitely mentioned.)

at the rear of Sang Hsien-ho and, taking him unawares, attacked and seriously defeated him. The morale of the troops was again restored. He was honored with the title of *kuang-lu ta-fu*.⁵¹

Turkish help alone, however, was not sufficient to enable the T'ang forces to reach Ch'ang-an. Li Yüan was, to be sure, immediately able to get the main body of his army across the Yellow River. After an unsuccessful attempt against the city of Ho-tung, he himself crossed over on October 17,⁵² and stopped at the Ch'ang-ch'un Palace.⁵³ Meanwhile, clever disposition of his forces was needed in order to prevent Ch'ü-t'u T'ung from circumventing his designs.

Among the many Sui officials who now joined the standard of the Duke of T'ang was the Magistrate of Hua-yin, Li Hsiao-ch'ang,⁵⁴ who came to surrender and placed Yung-fêng Granary at the disposal of the T'ang forces.⁵⁵ This district is strategically located just within the important pass of T'ung-kuan.

Before crossing the Yellow River, "Civil and military officers requested the Duke of T'ang to assume the duties of 'Grand Commandant'⁵⁶ and hence to establish the officials and assistants appertaining to this office. He followed this suggestion."⁵⁷ When he had thus increased his own prestige and that of his entourage, he sent out his armies by different routes all leading eventually to Ch'ang-an.

51. 光祿大夫, see Appendix D, n. 5. *Chiu T'ang-shu*, ch. 194B, p. 2a. In Chavannes, *Tou-kiue occidentaux*, p. 23, the phrase 諸軍復振 is wrongly translated "Quand les troupes furent de nouveau arrêtées ..." as if it were the beginning of the next sentence. Cf. *TCTC*, ch. 184, p. 10b.

52. 9th moon, day 57.

53. Ch'ang-ch'un kung 長春宮. *Chiu T'ang-shu*, ch. 1, p. 4a; *T'ang-shu*, ch. 1, p. 4b.

54. 李孝常. The name Li denotes that he may have been a clansman of Li Yüan.

55. *Chiu T'ang-shu*, ch. 1, p. 4a.

56. *T'ai-wei* 太尉, one of the "Three Dukes". See Appendix C.

57. 9th moon, day 55 (October 15, 617). *Chiu T'ang-shu*, ch. 1, p. 4a; *T'ang-shu*, ch. 1, p. 4b.

ADVANCE ON CH'ANG-AN

Li Chien-ch'êng, his eldest son, and Liu Wên-ching were sent
"to quarter troops at Yung-fêng Granary. Together they
guarded T'ung-kuan...."[58]
Ch'ü-t'u T'ung meanwhile had decided to go beyond the mountains to the south of Ch'ang-an and to relieve the capital from
that direction. "When his army reached T'ung-kuan it was
stopped by Liu Wên-ching and not able to advance. They were
deadlocked for over a month."[59] Thus Liu Wên-ching kept any
Sui force from the east from interfering with the Duke of T'ang's
advance.

When Li Yüan separated his forces, he sent Li Shih-min ahead
north of the Wei River and beyond to the west of Ch'ang-an
while he himself went more slowly by way of P'ing-i and Hsia-
kuei.[60] From all the countryside people flocked to meet them,
some leaders bringing thousands of reinforcements. Li Chien-
ch'êng was ordered to proceed south of the Wei to Pa-shang,[61]
southeast of Ch'ang-an and on an important route leading to
that city.[62]

Among those who helped this campaign by raising revolts on
their own account were relatives of the Duke of T'ang. His
cousin Li Shên-t'ung[63] and his daughter, the Lady Li, wife of a
man named Ch'ai Shao,[64] raised the standard of rebellion in the
districts directly to the west of Ch'ang-an and joined forces with

58. 9th moon, day 3 (October 23, 617). *Chiu T'ang-shu*, ch. 1, p.
4a. Cf. *T'ang-shu*, ch. 1, pp. 4b–5a.
59. *Chiu T'ang-shu*, ch. 59, p. 2b. See also *Chiu T'ang-shu*, ch. 57,
p. 8b; *T'ang-shu*, ch. 88, p. 3a, and ch. 89, pp. 2a–2b.
60. 下邽.
61. 霸上.
62. *Chiu T'ang-shu*, ch. 1, pp. 4a–4b, and ch. 2, p. 3a; *T'ang-shu*,
ch. 1, p. 5a, and ch. 2, p. 2b.
63. 李神通, d. 630. *CCBN*, p. 415. Biography in *Chiu T'ang-shu*,
ch. 60, and in *T'ang-shu*, ch. 78.
64. 柴紹妻李氏, later entitled Princess P'ing-yang 平陽公主, d.
623. *CCBN*, p. 191. Biography in *Chiu T'ang-shu*, ch. 58.

Li Shih-min when he arrived with the vanguard of the T'ang armies.[65]

Three weeks after the Duke of T'ang himself had crossed the Yellow River, he arrived outside the western capital.[66] His troops numbered some two hundred thousand.[67]

Within Ch'ang-an, as we have seen, the nominal chief was Yu, Prince of Tai, supported by a group of loyal officials. On his arrival, Li Yüan advised their surrender, but they refused and he proceeded to besiege the city. The defenders held out for five weeks, and finally, on December 12, 617,[68] after starvation had taken its toll among the populace, the Righteous Army entered Ch'ang-an in triumph.[69]

65. *Chiu T'ang-shu*, ch. 1, pp. 4a–4b; *TCTC*, ch. 184, pp. 13a–13b.
66. Ta-yeh 13th year, 10th moon, day 18 (November 7, 617).
67. *Chiu T'ang-shu*, ch. 1, p. 4b; *T'ang-shu*, ch. 1, p. 5a.
68. 11th moon, 9th day (day 53).
69. *Sui-shu*, ch. 4, p. 14b, and ch. 24, p. 20a; *Chiu T'ang-shu*. ch. 1, p. 4b; *T'ang-shu*, ch. 1, p. 5a.

XI. LI YÜAN'S POSITION, 617-618

Rivals Increase in Power

In order to understand the T'ang position at Ch'ang-an, it is well to keep in mind what happened in other sections of the country during the time of this campaign. Li Yüan and his followers were not the only ones who gained increased power and prestige.

Tou Chien-tê was now "King of Ch'ang-lo". During the years 617-618 he continued to expand his authority in the northeast at the expense of other rebels and officials still loyal to the Sui.[1]

In the central Yangtze valley another pretender to the throne appeared. Hsiao Hsien[2] was a relative of the Sui house and, more important still, a descendant of the Later Liang[3] dynasty, which had been overthrown by the Sui in 587. Set up by adherents of the old order as Duke of Liang, he moved to Pa-ling[4] (modern Yochow, Hunan) and later on was acclaimed by his followers as "King of Liang".[5]

To the northwest of the T'ang position Hsieh Chü controlled the main routes to Turkistan and had extended his authority into the upper Wei River valley. By September, 617, he felt himself powerful enough to lay claim to imperial dignity.[6] At about the

1. *Chiu T'ang-shu*, ch. 54, pp. 11b–12b.
2. 蕭銑, 583–621. *GBD* 703. *CCBN*, p. 1657. Biography in *Chiu T'ang-shu*, ch. 56, and in *T'ang-shu*, ch. 87 (Tr. Pfizmaier, "Gründung des Thang," pp. 46–52).
3. 後梁, 555–587; not to be confused with the dynasty of 907–923.
4. Pa-ling-chün 巴陵郡, present Yüeh-yang 岳陽 (Yüeh-chou 岳州).
5. Ta-yeh 13th year, 10th moon, day 33 (November 22, 617). *Sui-shu*, ch. 4, p. 14b; *Chiu T'ang-shu*, ch. 56, pp. 1a–2a; *TCTC*, ch. 184, pp. 15a–16a. Cf. *T'ang-shu*, ch. 1, p. 5a.
6. Ta-yeh 13th year, 7th moon (August 7–September 5, 617). *Chiu T'ang-shu*, ch. 55, p. 2a. Cf. *Sui-shu*, ch. 5, p. 2b.

same time in Wu-wei,[7] still further northwest, another Sui official, Li Kuei, threw off imperial authority and threatened Hsieh Chü's position by seizing the commanderies west of the Yellow River. Ta-tu-ch'üeh *shad*, the Western Turk chieftain who had for some years been at Hui-ning, was among those who joined forces with Li Kuei.[8]

To meet this opposition, Hsieh Chü sent troops across the Yellow River. They were defeated by a subordinate of Li Kuei, and Hsieh Chü moved his capital away from Chin-ch'eng. His son Hsieh Jên-kuo[9] was more successful in the southwest. When the latter had conquered T'ien-shui-chün[10] (known in T'ang and modern times as Ch'in-chou), Hsieh Chü transferred his capital there. Hsieh Jên-kuo advanced still further down the Wei River valley into Fu-fêng-chün. T'ang Pi was defeated and Hsieh Chü planned to continue to Ch'ang-an.[11] In this he was preceded by the Duke of T'ang.

Beyond the areas controlled by Hsieh Chü and Li Kuei, still further to the northwest at the frontier market city of Chang-yeh, from which only a few years before P'ei Chü supervised the trade routes to Central Asia, one more rebellion did away with some of the last vestiges of Sui authority.[12] With the exception of Hsieh Chü's advance towards Ch'ang-an, this and the other rebellions just mentioned had little effect on the T'ang leaders and their success in founding a dynasty. On the other hand, events in the region about Lo-yang were very significant.

7. Wu-wei-chün 武威郡, modern Liang-chou 涼州, recently changed again to Wu-wei.

8. *Sui-shu*, ch. 4, p. 14a; *Chiu T'ang-shu*, ch. 55, p. 5a; *T'ang-shu*, ch. 1, p. 4b.

9. 薛仁果 (usually written Jen-kao 仁杲; cf. *TCTC*, ch. 184, p. 19a), d. 618. *CCBN*, p. 1663. Biography in *Chiu T'ang-shu*, ch. 55, and in *T'ang-shu*, ch. 86 (Tr. Pfizmaier, "Aufstände gegen Sui," pp. 803–806). Concerning his name see also John C. Ferguson, "The Six Horses at the Tomb of the Emperor T'ai Tsung of the T'ang Dynasty," *Eastern Art*, Vol. III (1931), p. 64.

10. 天水郡, modern 秦州, recently changed again to T'ien-shui.

11. *Chiu T'ang-shu*, ch. 55, pp. 2a–2b.

12. Ta-yeh 13th year, 11th moon, day 12 (December 31, 617). *Sui-shu*, ch. 5, pp. 2a–2b.

Li Mi *vs.* Wang Shih-ch'ung

The rebellion of Li Mi continued to be one of the most important in helping to determine the fate of the Sui dynasty as well as that of the T'ang. In this same year, 617, Li Mi gained more adherents, both among former Sui officials and among rebel leaders. With the aid of some of them he was able in the autumn to seize the granary at Li-yang and thus to enlarge his sphere of control still further.[13]

Meanwhile, not far to the north, the Duke of T'ang was advancing towards Ch'ang-an. Li Mi considered· that he might obtain Li Yüan's aid for the extension of his own power; hence he wrote asking that they coöperate against the Sui. Li Mi at this time was in constant warfare against the Sui forces at the eastern capital, Lo-yang. The Duke of T'ang, however, merely sent him a courteous reply[14] and thus encouraged Li Mi while he carried out his own plans.

Li Mi and his opponent Wang Shih-ch'ung, whom Emperor Yang had especially commissioned to suppress him,[15] were occupied in continual fighting. During a period of about four months, over sixty engagements, large and small, were fought without distinct benefit to either side.[16] The struggle between the Sui forces and Li Mi was to the advantage of Li Yüan. He could proceed to organize his power in the Region within the Passes without fear of serious interference—at least for the time being.

13. 9th moon (October 6–November 3). *Sui-shu,* ch. 4, p. 14a. According to *T'ang-shu,* ch. 84, p. 5a, this event came before the 9th moon (see date p. 6a). *Chiu T'ang-shu,* ch. 53, seems to have a different sequence of events. *TCTC,* ch. 184, p. 9b, puts this after mention of 9th moon.

14. *T'ang-shu,* ch. 84, p. 6a, ... 作報書厚禮尊讓. 密大喜. ... Detailed accounts are given in *Chiu T'ang-shu,* ch. 53, and *CYCCC,* ch. 2, pp. 5b–7a.

15. Ta-yeh 13th year, 7th moon (August 7–September 5, 617). *TCTC,* ch. 184, pp. 3a–3b.

16. *Chiu T'ang-shu,* ch. 53, p. 13b, and *T'ang-shu,* ch. 84, pp. 16a–16b, give 60 plus in over 100 days. *Chiu T'ang-shu,* ch. 54, p. 2b, and *T'ang-shu,* ch. 85, p. 2b, give 100 plus.

T'ANG ORGANIZATION AT CH'ANG-AN

Immediately after entering Ch'ang-an, one of Li Yüan's first concerns was a new system of laws.

He ordered the Secretary in charge of the Official Tallies,[17] Sung Kung-pi[18] to collect the official documents[19] and to reduce the laws to twelve articles.[20]   Murderers, thieves and robbers, deserters from the army, and those who rebelled were to be put to death.[21]

The manner of this reorganization and the way in which historians have described it are in direct imitation of the records of what the founder of the Han dynasty accomplished when he first entered the Region within the Passes in 207 B.C.[22]

Thus even before the announcement of a new dynasty the traditions of a "proper" usurpation of power were complied with. The Duke of T'ang and his followers began at once to build up the legal and administrative organization which was to last for almost three hundred years and to become the basis of the laws of all nations within the sphere of Chinese culture.

Official changes also were undertaken soon after the seizure of the western capital.   Those who had led the active military resistance to the T'ang forces were put to death.[23]   On the last day of the cycle[24] Yang Yu, Prince of Tai, was set up as "Emperor".   "Emperor Yang was honored from afar as Grand

17. *Chu-fu-lang* 主符郎.
18. 宋公㢱.
19. *T'u chi* 圖籍 (lit. "charts and census records").
20. *T'iao* 條.
21. *T'ang-shu*, ch. 1, pp. 5a–5b.
22. Cf. Chavannes, *Mémoires historiques*, Vol. II, p. 353, and Dubs, *History of the Former Han Dynasty*, Vol. I, p. 58.   This following of a well-established precedent is noted in *Tzŭ-chih t'ung-chien kang-mu*, by Chu Hsi et al. (about 1190.   Published with commentaries by later writers, Shan-tung shu-chü, 1879), ch. 37, p. 11b.
23. *Chiu T'ang-shu*, ch. 1, p. 4b; *TCTC*, ch. 184, p. 16b.   Note, however, the exception made at Li Shih-min's request in favor of Li Ching 李靖; 571–649.   *GBD* 1112.   *CCBN*, pp. 436–437.   Biography in *Chiu T'ang-shu*, ch. 67; *T'ang-shu*, ch. 93; and in Amiot, "Portraits des célèbres Chinois," *Mém. conc. les Chinois*, Vol. V, pp. 202–228.
24. 11th moon, day 60 (December 19, 617).

Emperor",[25] the traditional title conferred upon an abdicating emperor. A general amnesty was declared and the reign title changed from Ta-yeh to I-ning.[26] Actual power was, of course, in the hands of Li Yüan, who on the next day, the first of the new cycle, was granted added titles. The chief ones were Great Chancellor[27] and Prince of T'ang.[28]

A few days later his three sons also received new titles. Li Chien-ch'êng was appointed Heir Apparent of the T'ang State,[29] Li Shih-min Grand Secretary[30] of the T'ang State and Duke of Ch'in,[31] and Li Yüan-chi Duke of Ch'i.[32]

During the next six months the ranks and privileges of all of them were gradually increased and new posts were created for various officials in preparation for the establishment of a new dynasty.[33] Of more actual importance was the military progress and the consequent strengthening of T'ang power.

25. *Yao tsun Yang-ti wei t'ai-shang-huang* 遙尊煬帝爲太上皇. *Chiu T'ang-shu*, ch. 1, p. 4b. In translating *t'ai-shang-huang* as "Grand Emperor" I am following the usage of Dubs, *History of the Former Han Dynasty*, Vol. I, p. 115. For a detailed study concerning the term *t'ai-shang* see Peter A. Boodberg, "Marginalia to the Histories of the Northern Dynasties," *Harvard Journal of Asiatic Studies*, Vol. III, Nos. 3 and 4 (December, 1938), pp. 235–238.

26. 義寧.

27. *Ta-ch'êng-hsiang* 大丞相. Des Rotours, *Le Traité des Examens*, p. 159, mentions this particular appointment and translates the title as "premier ministre". Dubs, *History of the Former Han Dynasty*, *passim*, translates *ch'êng-hsiang* as "Lieutenant Chancellor". The reason for not following the latter and translating "Great Lieutenant Chancellor" is that this would imply the existence of another and superior chancellor in the official hierarchy.

28. December 20, 617. *Sui-shu*, ch. 5, pp. 1a–2a; *Chiu T'ang-shu*, ch. 1, pp. 4b–5a; *T'ang-shu*, ch. 1, p. 5b.

29. 唐國世子.

30. *Nei-shih* 內史.

31.ʹ 秦公.

32. 齊公. 11th moon, day 6 (December 25, 617). *Sui-shu*, ch. 5, p. 2a. See also *Chiu T'ang-shu*, ch. 1, p. 5b, and ch. 2, p. 3a; *T'ang-shu*, ch. 1, p. 5b, and ch. 2, p. 2b. Duke of Ch'in and Duke of Ch'i are also written as Duke of the Ch'in State and Duke of the Ch'i State.

33. *Sui-shu*, ch. 5, p. 3a; *Chiu T'ang-shu*, ch. 1, p. 5b; *T'ang-shu*, ch. 1, pp. 5b–6a.

MILITARY CONSOLIDATION AND EXPANSION

Hsieh Chü's advance down the Wei River valley was the most direct threat to the newly established T'ang position at Ch'ang-an. To make the capital secure from that direction, Li Shih-min was appointed Field Marshal[34] and sent with an army to attack Hsieh Chü, January 8, 618.[35] Ten days later the Duke of Ch'in inflicted a crushing defeat and "decapitated several thousand men. He returned after pursuing the fugitives as far as the Lung-ch'ih [mountains or hills at the headwaters of the Wei River.]"[36]

At this same time Li Yüan's cousin, Li Hsiao-kung,[37] was sent south to occupy the Han River valley and before the end of the year other forces had aided the cause by the acquisition of the region of present Szechuan for Li Yüan.[38]

To the east T'ang arms had notable success. After about three months of struggle for control of T'ung-kuan, Liu Wên-ching was finally able to rout the Sui forces. He drove them back and took several tens of thousands of prisoners, including finally the Generalissimo[39] Ch'ü-t'u T'ung himself.[40]

Li Yüan then took advantage of this to send his sons Li Chien-ch'êng and Li Shih-min with some seventy thousand troops "to patrol the countryside in the direction of Lo-yang".[41] Li Shih-

34. *Yüan-shuai* 元帥.
35. Ta-yeh 13th year (617), 12th moon, day 20.
36. Lung-ch'ih 隴坻. *Chiu T'ang-shu*, ch. 55, p. 2b. See also *ibid.*, ch. 1, p. 5a; and *T'ang-shu*, ch. 86, p. 2a. *Chiu T'ang-shu*, ch. 2, pp. 3a-3b; and *T'ang-shu*, ch. 2, p. 2b, record that "more than ten thousand were decapitated".
37. 李孝恭, 591-640. *CCBN*, p. 393. Biography in *Chiu T'ang-shu*, ch. 60, and in *T'ang-shu*, ch. 78.
38. *Chiu T'ang-shu*, ch. 1, p. 5a, and ch. 60, p. 9a; *T'ang-shu*, ch. 1, p. 5b; *TCTC*, ch. 184, pp. 20a and 21b.
39. *Ta-chiang-chün* 大將軍.
40. Ta-yeh 13th year, 12th moon, day 34 (January 22, 618). *Sui-shu*, ch. 5, p. 2b. See also *Chiu T'ang-shu*, ch. 1, p. 5a; ch. 57, p. 8b; and ch. 59, pp. 2b-3b; *T'ang-shu*, ch. 88, p. 3a; and ch. 89, pp. 2a-2b.
41. *Chiu T'ang-shu*, ch. 1, pp. 5a-5b. See also *T'ang-shu*, ch. 1, p. 6a.

min "led ten thousand troops to attack Lo-yang, but without success. Hence he returned." A few miles southwest of Lo-yang, at San-wang-ling[42] he arranged a "triple ambush" and was thus enabled to defeat a Sui force of ten thousand men.[43]

Now that warfare had been successfully waged almost up to the gates of Lo-yang and all the territory west of it was under their control, the T'ang authorities were able to set up two prefectures (*chou*) for local administration directly west of the eastern capital. Li Shih-min was honored with the title of Duke of the Chao State.[44] He and his brother remained in the area with their troops for about three months until they were withdrawn in May 618.[45] In connection with this advance of the T'ang armies, it should be remembered that the principal Sui general, Wang Shih-ch'ung, and the main body of Sui forces at Lo-yang were engaged in an exhausting struggle with Li Mi to the north and east. In the preceding winter, the latter had inflicted a crushing defeat upon Wang's forces and was regarded by many as the most prominent leader in all of China.[46]

MURDER OF EMPEROR YANG

Military successes to the west, south, and east might well enable Li Yüan and his government at Ch'ang-an to disregard what was occurring in other parts of the country and to proceed with the founding of a new dynasty. But an event which occurred at Chiang-tu on April 11[47] must have greatly helped to give Li

42. 三王陵.
43. *T'ang-shu*, ch. 2, pp. 2b–3a. *Chiu T'ang-shu*, ch. 2, p. 3b, places these events in I-ning 1st year, 12th moon (January 2–31, 618).
44. 趙國公.
45. I-ning 2nd year, 4th moon, day 35 (May 23, 618). *Chiu T'ang-shu*, ch. 1, p. 5b, and ch. 2, p. 3b; *T'ang-shu*, ch. 1, p. 6a. Cf. *T'ang-shu*, ch. 2, p. 2b. The year is officially known as I-ning 2nd year up to 5th moon, day 1 (June 18, 618), and as Wu-tê 武德 1st year on and after 5th moon, day 1. See pp. 109 and 114.
46. I-ning 2nd year, 1st moon, day 59 (February 16, 618). *Sui-shu*, ch. 5, p. 2b; *Chiu T'ang-shu*, ch. 53, pp. 14b–15a, and ch. 54, p. 2b.
47. 3rd moon, day 53. *Sui-shu*, ch. 5, p. 2b; *Chiu T'ang-shu*, ch. 1, p. 5b; *T'ang-shu*, ch. 1, p. 6a.

Yüan's accession to the throne moral, if not legal, sanction in the eyes of his contemporaries. This was the murder of Emperor Yang in his palace near the Yangtze by a group of dissatisfied soldiers and officials headed by the General of the Right Garrison Guard[48] Yü-wên Hua-chi.[49] The latter was the son of Yü-wên Shu, the corrupt minister who had but recently died. Many of the Emperor's entourage were from the Region within the Passes and were not content to stay away from their homes, especially in such times as these. The spirit of revolt extended to the Emperor's own guard and those who remained loyal to him were powerless in the face of a carefully planned conspiracy.[50] Following the assassination of Emperor Yang, Yü-wên Hua-chi enthroned the dead Emperor's nephew, Yang Hao, another Prince of Ch'in,[51] as nominal ruler and set out for the north to compete with the other contenders for control of the country.

The disintegration of the Sui empire was now complete. All semblance of unity was gone. Rival war-lords temporarily supported puppet Sui "emperors" as a cloak of legitimacy to conceal their own struggle for personal advantage. Comparable with the actions of Li Yüan at Ch'ang-an and Yü-wên Hua-chi at Chiang-tu was that of Wang Shih-ch'ung and other Sui officials at Lo-yang in their support of Emperor Yang's grandson, the Prince of Yüeh,[52] as legitimate successor to the throne. None of the three "emperors," however was considered as more than a nominal ruler. China was ready for another dynasty to replace the Sui.

48. *Yu-t'un-wei chiang-chün* 右屯衛將軍.
49. 宇文化及, d. 619. *GBD* 2535. *CCBN*, p. 239. Biography in *Sui-shu*, ch. 85 (Tr. Pfizmaier, "Fortsetzungen ... des Hauses Sui," pp. 249–259), and in *Pei-shih*, ch. 79.
50. *Sui-shu*, ch. 85, pp. 2a–4b.
51. 秦王, personal name Yang Hao 楊浩, d. 618. *CCBN*, p. 1271. Biographical information in *Sui-shu*, ch. 45, pp. 13b–14a; ch. 5, p. 3a; *Pei-shih*, ch. 71, p. 8b; and *Chiu T'ang-shu*, ch. 1, p. 8b.
52. 越王, personal name Yang T'ung 楊侗, later known as Kung-ti 恭帝, d. 619. *CCBN*, p. 1214. Biography in *Sui-shu*, ch. 59, and in *Pei-shih*, ch. 71. He was enthroned at Lo-yang just after Li Yüan's accession at Ch'ang-an. *Chiu T'ang-shu*, ch. 1, p. 7a; *T'ang-shu*, ch. 1, p. 6b.

DIPLOMACY AND ACCESSION OF LI YÜAN

At Ch'ang-an, Li Yüan continually gained new adherents. Mention has been made of the conquests carried out by his subordinates to the east, south, and west. In the north also his sphere of influence was increased. Of especial importance among those who joined the T'ang cause, after the death of Emperor Yang, were some of the leaders who controlled territories in and near the Ordos region within the great bend of the Yellow River. One of these, Chang Ch'ang-hsün, has been mentioned as adhering to the Turks with his commandery, Wu-yüan-chün. To the north of him was a prominent leader of the Eastern Turks, entitled Baghatur *shad*,[53] who was to become the most formidable foreign foe of the T'ang dynasty during the next decade. Both Hsieh Chü and Li Yüan desired the Turk's support in their rivalry for supremacy in the northwest. The T'ang envoys succeeded, partly through bribery and partly because Chang Ch'ang-hsün joined the cause of Li Yüan. The Turk was kept from aiding Hsieh Chü at a time when such an alliance might have been fatal to the T'ang.[54]

The stage was now nearly ready for Li Yüan's accession to the throne. During the six months since his entrance into Ch'ang-an, T'ang arms and diplomacy had insured control not only of modern Shensi province and parts of Shansi and Kansu, but also of territories beyond the eastern and northern boundaries of the Region within the Passes. T'ang authority encroached on Lo-yang beyond T'ung-kuan and satisfactory terms had been made with the Turks to the north. Furthermore, as Prince of T'ang, Li Yüan had been "granted" successively higher honors by the nominal Sui ruler. The rest was a matter of form. On June 12, 618[55] Yang Yu abdicated the throne at Ch'ang-an. The imperial insignia was offered to Li Yüan. Again he followed

53. Mo-ho-tu *shê* 莫賀咄設, personal name Tu-pi 咄苾 later known as Hsieh-li Khan 頡利可汗, d. 634. Biography in *Chiu T'ang-shu*, ch. 194A, and in *T'ang-shu*, ch. 215.

54. *Chiu T'ang-shu*, ch. 55, p. 2b; ch. 57, pp. 17a–17b; 194A, pp. 2b–3a; *T'ang-shu*, ch. 1, p. 6a; *TCTC*, ch. 185, pp. 10a–10b.

55. I-ning 2nd year, 5th moon, day 55.

ancient precedent[56] by thrice refusing and finally accepting the honor.   Then six days later, on the first day of a new cycle,[57] he formally ascended the throne, proclaimed a general amnesty and changed the reign title from I-ning to Wu-tê.[58]   This was the official beginning of the great T'ang dynasty which continued to be the ruling house of China until 907.

56. Cf. Chavannes, *Mémoires historiques*, Vol. II, p. 380.
57. 5th moon, day 1 (June 18, 618).
58. *Sui-shu*, ch. 5, pp. 3a–4a; *Chiu T'ang-shu*, ch. 1, pp. 5b–6b; *T'ang-shu*, ch. 1, p. 16b.

XII. CONCLUSION

END OF THE SUI

The period of change from the Sui dynasty to the T'ang may be divided into three separate phases: the decline and end of the old empire, the growth of various new and shifting centers of power, and the attainment by one of these of an especially favorable position among the rest. Unrelated as their details may appear to be, they constitute one continuous story and must be so considered if the significance of each is to be understood.

The fall of the Sui dynasty has been attributed to Emperor Wên's change of the succession and to the weakness and incompetency of Emperor Yang. In the preceding chapters the writer has tried to show that the latter's character has often been misinterpreted. His constant attention to frontier affairs, his promotion of trade and his territorial extension of the empire may have been unwise and at times were certainly carried forward with a ruthless energy which greatly contributed to their failure. But they are not the behavior of a pleasure-loving madman and seem to have much of serious purpose behind them. It must be constantly kept in mind that the Chinese records were handed down by scholars most unfavorable to Emperor Yang and desirous of glorifying their own rulers, the T'ang, at his expense.

It should not be considered that the Li family supplanted Emperor Yang through superior skill or merit of their own. His empire collapsed through causes for which the following dynasty was in no way responsible. The T'ang leaders merely took advantage of the fact that the Sui empire was already in process of disintegration. Li Yüan was not even one of the most important officials of the Sui. Much less did he and his party have any opportunity of matching their ability against the Sui empire at its height.

The year 610 may be taken as the approximate time of Emperor Yang's greatest power. He had for some years enjoyed a

115

new and resplendent capital at Lo-yang. His northern frontier
was protected by strengthened fortifications along the line of the
Great Wall. Hard labor had linked the waterways of north and
central China to form a new line for imperial communications
and commerce. Many lives and much treasure had been ex-
pended to enlarge the borders of the empire until they reached
down the coast of Indo-China and to the oases of Turkistan.
Yet in the official annals for the years 608 to 612 there are no
references to anything approaching serious or widespread rebellion.

This makes it all the more remarkable that within a few years
the empire should be torn with civil strife. The history of
Emperor Yang's ambition, leading him on to disastrous foreign
ventures, has been traced in the foregoing chapters. "East of
the Mountains," where lasting disaffection started at the time
of the Korean campaigns, the pressure of military conscription
was aggravated by flood and later by drought.

Emperor Yang does not seem to have known when to stop in
the face of military checks and adverse natural conditions. His
persistence may have been the sign of an unbalanced mind.
Since his campaign against the southern empire of Ch'ên in his
early years, he had known little of failure and in his reign as
Emperor the campaign of 612 marks his first serious reverse.
He continued to wage war against Koguryŏ and after the start
of serious rebellions in 613 was incapable of recovering his former
prestige and power.

Yang Hsüan-kan's uprising came in 613. For the years that
follow we hear much of Tou Chien-tê, Li Mi, and others who
gathered numbers of followers in opposition to the government.
We know of their influence and prestige, but cannot be entirely
sure concerning the forces responsible for the events of the period.
The records give little direct information in regard to the various
parties, factions, or secret societies which may have guided the
Emperor and the happenings of his time to a greater extent than
we now know.

His extensive travels from Kansu in one direction, to the Liao
River in the other, and from Chiang-tu in the south to Yen-mên

in the north make us realize that the Emperor was personally interested in state affairs. Other considerations point to the same conclusion. And yet, further research may perhaps disclose definite cliques of officials who were encouraging or opposing these undertakings. The literati seem to have thought little of them, since they wrote about them chiefly as a disparagement to Emperor Yang. His public works were criticized from the point of view of extravagance, waste of men and money. The fact that emphasis is placed on this phase of these undertakings suggests that others opposed to the literati were profiting at their expense. The tendency of Emperor Yang to favor southern ideas has already been referred to and may be a clue to forces which worked against each other within the administration. Yang Hsüan-kan's rebellion is an example of a wide breach within the ranks of the official class. There is little in his biography, however, to indicate just how and why the factional differences developed to an extent where some of the officials were ready to break with the Emperor and to help Yang Hsüan-kan in his ambitions.

From other sources, we gain information which may help to form an hypothesis on this subject. The statements of Tou Chien-tê and the development of other later rebellions lead to the conclusion that, regardless of its success in unifying the country and regardless of the increase in imperial prestige and power, the Sui dynasty did not really succeed in winning the loyalty of the Chinese. Since the days of the Han dynasty, men had been too much accustomed to change of rulers and to constant shifting of political forces for them to think in terms of a stable dynasty, an emperor who was really "Son of Heaven". Furthermore, the possible benefits of a unified country were disregarded in favor of local interests. Traditions of regional independence had become so intrenched that men readily turned to the leaders who represented these traditions in a time of crisis. Adventurous men throughout the land thought that they might be emperor of at least part of China and perhaps of the whole country. Only with the advent of extremely able leaders, Li Yüan and Li Shih-min, did the Chinese regain the feeling of imperial majesty and of recognized authority.

The feeling of instability may have been easily aggravated by popular superstitions and thus used by factions or secret organizations to promote their own ends. Such seems probable in the case of the ballad or catch regarding the rise of the Li family. This popular saying is most interesting as directly linking the fate of the two imperial houses.[1]

The ballad, which probably originated among the followers of Li Mi, was recounted to Emperor Yang by a soothsayer, very likely a Taoist. It was then used by the enemies of Li Hun in order to turn the Emperor against him and only later did it come to be connected with the fortunes of the Duke of T'ang. May it not be that members of the Li clan in association with Taoists who hoped to profit by their rise to power took advantage of the unrest at the time of the Korean campaigns, which they realized might well result in a change of dynasty, to spread this rumor among a superstitious populace? With this rumor a Taoist had helped Emperor Yang against Li Hun, it is true, but they must have been aware of the advantages which might come to them from the accession of a Li to imperial power. In support of this theory it should be noted that Li Yüan, as Emperor, favored the Taoists and claimed descent from Lao-tzŭ, traditionally associated with the Li clan. It is possible that this later support was partly in recognition of their aid in earlier years.

In any case prominent men of the Li name throughout the country seem to have gained by the telling of the ballad and the Sui dynasty to have lost proportionately in the popular estimation. Li Mi was long a favorite while Li Yüan and his party were strengthened by the singing of this prophetic catch. Among minor rebels named Li, Li Hung was set up as "emperor" in 614 and later the former Sui official Li Kuei was given first place by his fellow insurgents at Wu-wei on account of his surname. When serious insurrection within and loss of prestige abroad had weakened the position of the dynasty, men would naturally turn

1. See especially the version in *Chiu T'ang-shu*, ch. 37, p. 30a.

to whomsoever else might in any way offer them hope of security
and advancement.

Beginning of the T'ang

In considering the various rebellious movements which existed
at the beginning of 617, we have already noted what were some of
the advantages enjoyed by the Duke of T'ang in T'ai-yüan
before he or his partisans began to revolt.[2] By the end of 617
Li Yüan and his followers were established at the western capital,
had set up a nominal emperor to give legitimacy to their usurpation of authority and may be considered to have reached a
position of preëminence among the various contenders.

In the first place, their geographical situation was more favorable than that of any of their rivals. The strategic importance
of the Region within the Passes has been emphasized more than
once in the preceding pages. This area, controlling the routes
to the west and protected by mountain ranges from the rest of
China, was firmly held as the center of T'ang power. The one
region to the east which had easy access to their territory, the
present province of Shansi, was held by T'ang forces, at least as
far north as T'ai-yüan. T'ang control was established not only
over the narrow pass of T'ung-kuan, but also over the territories
directly beyond it. To the west Hsieh Chü had been routed and
driven back to the headwaters of the Wei, while far to the north
in the Ordos T'ang adherents helped to prevent the Turks from
combining with other forces against Li Yüan. To the south of
the Region within the Passes are the high ranges of the Ch'in-ling,
a formidable natural barrier. Soon after Ch'ang-an had been
taken, however, T'ang influence was extended beyond those
mountains to include much of the Han River valley and part of
modern Szechuan.

These areas would hardly have been gained were it not for the
men who were leading the T'ang movement, Li Yüan and Li
Shih-min. From the time of his taking control in T'ai-yüan,
the Duke of T'ang had been a central figure about whom ambi-

2. See pp. 80–81.

tious and able men had gathered. He had shown himself a capable leader in the service of the Sui dynasty and appears to have been the sort of man to whom others instinctively turned in a time of emergency. Some accounts would lead one to believè that other men used Li Yüan to further their own ends. It must be admitted that without the skillful aid of others he would not have succeeded. It is difficult to disassociate the man and the movement. But, whether we incline towards those who chiefly favor his son, Li Shih-min, or whether we give first place to the father in evaluating the T'ang uprising, we cannot disregard the fact that the Duke of T'ang was the one to whom the others of his party looked up as their chief.

The principal question lies in comparing the relative importance of Li Yüan and Li Shih-min as founders of the dynasty. By his later military successes, and by his excellence as Emperor, the son eclipsed his father as an outstanding figure in Chinese history. Furthermore, he took especial pains to patronize the Confucian scholars, the very men who were writing the history of his early years, and handing down those records of his dynasty on which the standard histories of the T'ang period are based. Li Yüan seems to have been cautious and unimaginative in comparison with Li Shih-min. This impression is gained from the accounts in the dynastic histories as to the beginnings of revolt at T'ai-yüan and the campaign from there to Ch'ang-an. On the other hand, Wên Ta-ya, who was official recorder at the Duke of T'ang's headquarters during these events, describes Li Yüan as the real leader and gives little to indicate that Li Shih-min was especially important. In the case of each of these two conflicting versions, it seems probable that the importance of one man was magnified at the expense of the other. Further research is needed before a conclusion can be reached in regard to the details. But this much seems evident: those from whose records the dynastic histories were written tried as much as possible to honor their hero T'ai-tsung (Li Shih-min) and hence, either minimized Li Yüan's importance in order better to display the talents of his son, or accomplished the same result by depicting the founders of the dynasty according to a classical literary pattern.

The present writer has aimed, therefore, merely to give a simple outline of Li Yüan's achievements in starting the T'ang dynasty, realizing at the same time that his success may have been due largely to the able men who joined his cause—their very adherence, however, being a sign of his leadership.

In this study Li Shih-min is important chiefly as he participated in the events of 615-618 up to the time of the accession of his father to the throne. His great military achievements lay in the years immediately following this event, and were of sufficient brilliance to assure him rank among the best generals in Chinese history. It does not detract from his greatness as a general or as a statesman to doubt some of the stories concerning his early career which appear in the dynastic histories. Two in particular have been noted as possibly of doubtful value. The first, included by Ssŭ-ma Kuang in his narrative, concerns the siege of Yen-mên and Li Shih-min's advice to the relieving general Yün Ting-hsing, in whose biography no mention is made of any such relief. The second case is that of the critical battle of Yin-ma Spring where cavalry of the Western Turk, Ta-nai, saved the day for T'ang, for which Li Shih-min's biography gives him the whole credit. Again in both these instances, it is difficult to disassociate the man from the movement. These stories may have a basis of fact, and yet they make us wonder whether Li Shih-min's share in the rebellion in T'ai-yüan has not also been exaggerated.

The Duke of T'ang was surrounded from the start by men who later proved to be very capable in the affairs of the empire. Taken as a whole, Li Yüan, Li Shih-min, the latter's sister and other relatives who aided their cause in the Region within the Passes, together with various men of high and low rank who joined them, constituted a strong party. It seems unlikely that the scheme for rebellion and independent action was due to any one man, whether Liu Wên-ching, Li Shih-min or another. The prophecy concerning the Li family was on men's lips and must have occurred to all Li Yüan's following as a possibility. If the origin of the movement may be traced to certain individuals other than Li Yüan himself, the writer believes that either a group of scholars, including Wên Ta-ya, was responsible and, concealing their share, gave the chief credit to Li Yüan, or else that Liu Wên-ching, a man of an older generation than Li Shih-min, used the latter's youthful enthusiasm and daring to arouse others who had already been attracted by the leadership and prestige of the Duke of T'ang.

These leaders and this party, strong as they were, would not have succeeded had they not fully utilized the advantages at hand. The geographical advantage has already been stressed. Other prominent leaders who had proclaimed their independence by 617 were either remote from the capital or were contending on the north China plain in an exhausting struggle against one another or against those remaining loyal to the Sui. Li Mi seemed to many to be the most likely to succeed. It is to the credit of Li Yüan and his party that during their campaign they kept on friendly terms with Li Mi and thus prevented his interfering with their plans, but at the same time did not allow themselves to be drawn down on to the plains and away from the conquest of the Region within the Passes. They later sent troops to help against the Sui stronghold at Lo-yang, but only after they had firmly established themselves at Ch'ang-an.

The T'ang party also used Turkish aid to the best advantage. The Western Turk Ta-nai had settled with his tribe at Lou-fan, in Shansi, probably a little before Li Yüan started suppressing banditry in that region in 615. They were then both loyal supporters of Emperor Yang. After the latter's retirement to Chiang-tu in 616 it seems likely that they worked together on more than one occasion in establishing order in the region. At any rate, Ta-nai was with Li Yüan at the start of his campaign and subsequently rendered invaluable service to the cause.

The Duke of T'ang's relations with the Eastern Turks presents a different problem and one which needs further research, including a study of Wên Ta-ya's account and the history of Sino-Turkish relations throughout Li Yüan's reign as Emperor. While we know that he fought successfully against them in 616, they in turn defeated his men in the following year. They can scarcely be considered as belonging to his "party", and yet Li Yüan needed their aid, especially in the matter of cavalry and horses, if he were to be successful against the Sui forces on his way to Ch'ang-an. Shih-pi Khan was ready to take advantage of any movement which might extend his sphere of influence. Hence he bestowed titles on rebels in the Ordos and was in friendly relations with others to the east of modern Shansi. Both the Turkish Khan and Li Yüan stood to gain from an agreement whereby one should help the other against Emperor Yang. Horses and mounted warriors were to be exchanged for silk and treasure. The two were united in a common cause against the Emperor. Although he acted independently, Li Yüan was still nominally loyal to the dynasty and asked Shih-pi's aid that they might coöperate in restoring order to the Sui state. The Khan undoubtedly realized the ambitions of the T'ang party, but he may have been glad to aid their forces, including Ta-nai's Western Turks, in going farther from his borders. Whatever was the exact relationship between Shih-pi and Li Yüan, the latter showed great skill in using the Turks to gain his own ends. Their aid guaranteed the success of his expedition and the military expansion which followed.

With a strong party supporting him in his control of the capital and Turkish aid contributing to military victories beyond the passes, Li Yüan was in a position of real authority. Success followed on success and the new dynasty gradually gained control of the empire.

APPENDIX A

CHRONOLOGY[1]

Western Dates	Chinese Dates	Important Events
(581)[2]	K'ai-huang 1st year	End of Northern Chou dynasty, 1st year of Sui Wên-ti
(589)	" 9th "	End of Ch'ên dynasty. Sui supreme throughout China
(598)	" 18th "	
599 , January 1st	" " , 11th moon, 29th day, (day 33)[3]	
599 , " 23rd	" " , 12th moon, 22nd day, (day 55)	Birth of Li Shih-min
(599)	" 19th "	
(600)	" 20th "	
(601)	Jên-shou 1st year	
604 , August 13th	" 4th " , 7th moon, 13th day, (day 44)	Death of Sui Wên-ti
(605)	Ta-yeh 1st year	1st year of Sui Yang-ti
612 , February 7th to March 7th	" 8th " , 1st moon	Military assembly at Cho-chün, start of campaigns against Koguryŏ
613 , June 25th	" 9th " , 6th moon, 3rd day, (day 42)	Yang Hsüan-kan rebelled
614 , January 1st	" " " , 11th moon, 15th day, (day 52)	
614 , September 7th	" 10th " , 7th moon, 28th day, (day 1)	"Submission" of Koguryŏ
615 , January 1st	" " " , 11th moon, 26th day (day 57)	
615 , September 11th to October 12th	" 11th " , 8th moon, 13th day (day 10) to 9th moon, 15th day (day 41)	Yang-ti besieged at Yen-mên
616 , January 1st	" " , 12th moon, 7th day (day 2)	
616 , August 27th	" 12th " , 7th moon, 10th day (day 1)	Yang-ti left Lo-yang for Chiang-tu

Year	Western date	Reign	Chinese date (cyclical day)	Event
617	January 1st	" " "	11th moon, 19th day (day 8)	Sui officials seized by Li Yüan
617	June 23rd	" " 13th "	5th moon, 15th day (day 1)	
617	December 12th	" " "	11th moon, 9th day (day 53)	Li Yüan took Ch'ang-an
617	December 19th	" " "	11th moon, 16th day (day 60)	Yang Yu made "emperor"
617	December 20th	I-ning 1st year	11th moon, 17th day (day 1)	New reign period, 1st year of Sui Kung-ti. Li Yüan, Prince of T'ang
618	January 1st	" " "	11th moon, 29th day (day 13)	
618	April 11th	" " 2nd "	3rd moon, 11th day (day 53)	Murder of Yang-ti
618	June 12th	" " "	5th moon, 14th day (day 55)	Resignation of Sui Kung-ti
618	June 18th	Wu-tê 1st year	5th moon, 20th day (day 1)	Li Yüan, Emperor. New reign period, 1st year of T'ang Kao-tsu.

1. In making this chronological correspondence table reference has been made to the annals of the following dynastic histories: *Sui-shu*, *Pei-shih*, *Chiu T'ang-shu*, and *T'ang-shu*. Two western works have been used: Pierre Hoang, *Concordance des Chronologies Néoméniques Chinoise et Européenne. Variétés Sinologiques No. 29* (Shanghai, 1910) and Mathias Tchang, *Synchronismes Chinois: Chronologie Complète et Concordance avec l'Ère Chrétienne de toutes les dates concernant l'histoire de l'Extrême-Orient (Chine, Japon, Corée, Annam, Mongolie, etc.) (2357 av. J.-C.—1904 apr. J.-C.). Variétés Sinologiques No. 24* (Shanghai, 1905).

2. Western years approximately equivalent to the adjoining Chinese years are indicated in parenthesis.

3. Cyclical dates are indicated in parenthesis.

APPENDIX B

GENEALOGICAL TABLE

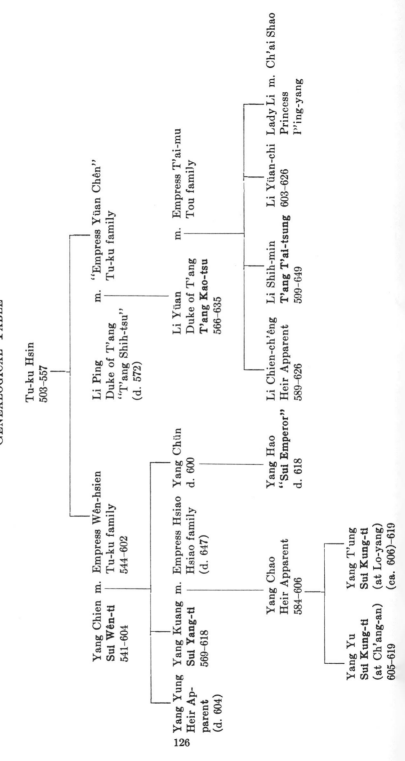

Tu-ku Hsin
503–557

Yang Chien m. Empress Wên-hsien
Sui Wên-ti   Tu-ku family
541–604   544–602

Yang Yung
Heir Ap-
parent
(d. 604)

Yang Kuang m. Empress Hsiao
Sui Yang-ti   Hsiao family
569–618   (d. 647)

Yang Chün
d. 600

Yang Chao
Heir Apparent
584–606

Yang Yu
Sui Kung-ti
(at Ch'ang-an)
605–619

Yang T'ung
Sui Kung-ti
(at Lo-yang)
(ca. 606)–619

"Empress Yüan Chên"
Tu-ku family

m.

Li Ping
Duke of T'ang
"T'ang Shih-tsu"
(d. 572)

Li Yüan
Duke of T'ang
T'ang Kao-tsu
566–635

m. Empress T'ai-mu
Tou family

Yang Hao
"Sui Emperor"
d. 618

Li Chien-ch'êng
Heir Apparent
589–626

Li Shih-min
T'ang T'ai-tsung
599–649

Li Yüan-chi
603–626

Lady Li m. Ch'ai Shao
Princess
P'ing-yang

APPENDIX C

OUTLINE OF SUI GOVERNMENT, 607–618

A description of the governmental system of Sui times, together with the changes occurring during the dynasty, is given in *Sui-shu*, ch. 28, part of the "Monograph on the Hundred Officials" (*Pai-kuan chih* 百官志), *Sui-shu*, ch. 26–28. No western translation of this *chüan* exists. It should be noted that the Sui system was essentially the same as that of former dynasties and in turn became the model for the T'ang rulers. At the beginning of the first chapter on officials in the *T'ang-shu*, it is stated: "In the regulations for T'ang officials, names, titles, salaries, and appointments, although they fluctuated with the times, yet generally speaking all continued the old Sui system."[1] Fortunately this T'ang governmental system has been carefully worked out by Robert Des Rotours in "Les grands fonctionnaires des provinces en Chine sous la dynastie des T'ang," *TP* 2nd Series, Vol. XXV (1927), pp. 219–332, and in his introduction to *Le Traité des Examens traduit de la Nouvelle Histoire des T'ang (Chap. XLIV, XLV)*, Bibliothèque de l'Institut des Hautes Études Chinoises, Vol. II, (Paris 1932). Hence the reader's attention is directed to these works for a more comprehensive summary of the Chinese government in the seventh century than is here presented.

The Chinese government, as it existed at the time of Emperor Wên's death and Emperor Yang's accession to the throne (604), was made up of a hierarchy of officials with varying degrees of rank and in many cases with elaborate honorary titles, many of them difficult or impossible of translation.[2] This organization was in large measure taken over by Emperor Yang. Certain changes were made, however, some of which have already been noted.[3] The following outline, based on *Sui-shu*, ch. 28, includes the principal divisions of the central government as they were after the changes of May 15, 607, the date on which the changes were officially recorded as being in effect.[4]

1. *T'ang-shu*, ch. 46, p. 1a.
2. *Sui-shu*, ch. 28, pp. 1a–21a, gives the system of Emperor Wên. *Ibid.*, ch. 28, pp. 21a–22b, gives the changes made during his reign.
3. See above, pp. 11–12.
4. Ta-yeh 3rd year, 4th moon, day 29. *Sui-shu*, ch. 3, p. 8b. See also *ibid.*, ch. 28, pp. 22b–33a, for the governmental changes of 607; synopsis in *TCTC*, ch. 180, p. 17a.

127

Honorary Advisory Positions
The Three Dukes,	*san-kung*, 三公
(The Three Preceptors, abolished in 607.)	*san-shih*, 三師

Civil Administration
Department of State Affairs (or Inner Cabinet),	*shang-shu-shêng*, 尙書省
Six Boards,	*liu-pu*, 六部
Board of Civil Office,	*li-pu*, 吏部
Board of Rites,	*li-pu*, 禮部
Board of War,	*ping-pu*, 兵部
Board of Justice,	*hsing-pu*, 刑部
Board of Public Revenues,	*min-pu*, 民部 or *hu-pu*, 戶部
Board of Public Works,	*kung-pu*, 工部
Department of the Imperial Chancellery,	*mên-hsia-shêng*, 門下省
Department of the Grand Imperial Secretariat,	*nei-shih-shêng*, 內史省
Department of the Imperial Library,	*mi-shu-shêng*, 祕書省
Department of the Imperial Domestic Service,	*tien-nei-shêng*, 殿內省
Tribunate of the Censors,	*yü-shih-t'ai*, 御史臺
Tribunate of Imperial Ushers,	*yeh-chê-t'ai*, 謁者臺
Tribunate of Imperial Police,	*ssŭ-li-t'ai*, 司隸臺
Court of Imperial Sacrifices,	*t'ai-ch'ang-ssŭ*, 太常寺
Court of Imperial Banquets,	*kuang-lu-ssŭ*, 光祿寺
Court of Imperial Insignia,	*wei-wei-ssŭ*, 衞尉寺
Court of Affairs of the Imperial Family,	*tsung-chêng-ssŭ*, 宗正寺
Court of Imperial Equipage,	*t'ai-p'u-ssŭ*, 太僕寺
Supreme Court of Justice,	*ta-li-ssŭ*, 大理寺
Court of Ceremonial towards Foreigners,	*hung-lu-ssŭ*, 鴻臚寺
Court of Agricultural Control,	*ssŭ-nung-ssŭ*, 司農寺
Court of Imperial Treasure,	*t'ai-fu-ssŭ*, 太府寺
Administration of Imperial Workshops,	*shao-fu-chien*, 少府監
Administration of the Inner Palace,	*ch'ang-ch'iu-chien*, 長秋監 (formerly *nei-shih-shêng*, 內侍省)
Administration of the Imperial Academy,	*kuo-tzŭ-chien*, 國子監

Administration of Works,   *chiang-tso-chien,* 將作監

Administration of Water-Con-   *tu-shui-chien,* 都水監
trol,

Military Administration

Left and Right Wing Guards,   *tso-yu-i-wei,* 左右翊衛

Left and Right Mounted Guards-   *tso-yu-ch'i-wei,* 左右騎尉
men,

Left and Right Martial (or   *tso-yu-wu-wei,* 左右武衛
Armed) Guards,

Left and Right Garrison Guards,   *tso-yu-t'un-wei,* 左右屯衛

Left and Right Defense Guards,   *tso-yu-yü-wei,* 左右禦衛

Left and Right Archer Guards,   *tso-yu-hou-wei,* 左右候衛

Left and Right Palace Watch,   *tso-yu-pei-shên-fu,* 左右備身府

Left and Right Gate Watch,   *tso-yu-chien-mên-fu,* 左右監門府

APPENDIX D

Uprisings, 613–617

Chronology of outbreaks of banditry and rebellion from Ta-yeh 9th year (613) to 13th year (617), 5th moon; including a few dates of other events of primary importance, translated from the annals of the Sui dynasty, *Sui-shu*, ch. 4, with references to the *Pei-shih* and the *Tzŭ-chih t'ung-chien*.[1]

Sui-Shu, [Ta-yeh] 9th year [613] . . . 1st moon, . . . day 19 [February 2], the
ch. 4, p. 5b bandit leaders Tu Yen-ping 杜彥冰 [*Pei-shih*, ch. 12, p. 9a, gives *yung* 永 for *ping*], Wang Jun 王潤 and others overthrew P'ing-yüan-chün 平原郡 [II, 3I];[2] [after] great plunder they left. . . .

Day 32 [February 15], Li Tê-i 李德逸 of P'ing-yüan collected a host of several ten thousand. [He was] called the A-chiu bandit 阿舅賊 and [he] robbed and plundered East of the Mountains 山東. Pai Yü-wang 白榆妄 [*TCTC*, ch. 182, p. 1a, reads 瑜娑 Yü-(so?)], [bandit leader] of Ling-wu 靈武 [2C], called the "slave bandit" 奴賊 robbed and plundered the horses that were being pastured and turned north to join the Turks. Lung-yu 隴右 [T'ang province, *tao* 道, in northwestern Kansu] suffered greatly from his evil 患. [The Emperor] sent the general Fan Kuei 范貴 to punish them. Throughout the year and into the next he had not been able to overcome [them]. [Cf. *Sui-shu*, ch. 24, p. 19b.] . . .

p. 6a 2nd moon, day 56 [March 11], Han Chin-lo 韓進洛, a man of Chi-pei

1. References to the biographies from which much of the material in the *TCTC* is taken are given in footnotes in the main chapters of this study.

2. Place names may be located by direct reference to the maps at the end of this volume. Characters for the name and map reference numbers (for places shown on Map II) are given only at the first mention in this translation. For the modern equivalents of the more important places see references throughout the main chapters of this study. The Sui names are given here just as they appear in the Chinese. Most of them refer to commanderies whether or not they include the suffix, which means "commandery", i.e. *chün*. In both cases sometimes the administrative area and sometimes the capital city of the area is meant. That is to say, the capital city of the commandery may be identified with the territory of that name. For example see below (p. 132) the translation from *Sui-shu* ch. 4. p. 7a: "Lü Ming-hsing led a host . . . to besiege Tung-chün." He could not have besieged the whole area. In this case at least, the suffix *chün* is used as part of the name of a city. On the maps all commanderies are marked as *chün* and are located at the administrative center of each, the capital city of the commandery. In some cases the name of the district (*hsien*) has also been added.

濟北 [II, 3I], gathered a host of several ten thousand as a company of robbers. . . .

3rd moon, day 13 [March 28], Mêng Hai-kung 孟海公, a man of Chi-yin 濟陰 [II, 4H] [*Pei-shih*, ch. 12, reads Chi-pei], raised troops [in revolt] to become robbers. [His] host reached several ten thousand. . . .

Day 37 [April 21], Kuo Fang-ting 郭方頂 [*Pei-shih*, ch. 12, reads Fang-yü 方預], a man of Pei-hai 北海 [II, 3J], gathered followers as robbers and styled himself Duke of Lu 盧公. [His] host reached thirty thousand. He attacked and overthrew the commandery [*chün*] city [i.e. I-tu 益都, II, 3J]; [after] great plunder he left. . . .

5th moon, day 16 [May 30], Chên Pao-ch'ê 甄寶車, a man of Chi-pei, gathered a host of over ten thousand; [they] raided and plundered the towns [of that region].

6th moon, day 42 [June 25], Yang Hsüan-kan 楊玄感 rebelled at Li-yang 黎陽 [II, 4H]. . . .

7th moon, . . . day 20 [August 2], Liu Yüan-chin 劉元進, a man of Yü-hang 餘杭 [II, 7K], raised troops in rebellion. [His] host reached several ten thousand.   p. 6b

8th moon, day 39 [August 21], the Generalissimo of the Left Wing Guard [*tso-i-wei ta-chiang-chün* 左翊衛大將軍] Yü-wên Shu 宇文述 and others defeated Yang Hsüan-kan at Wên-hsiang 閱鄉 [II, 5F] and decapitated him. The remainder of his party were all pacified.

Day 40 [August 22], Chu Hsieh 朱燮, a man of Wu 吳 [*TCTC*, ch. 182, p. 11a, reads Wu-chün 吳郡. II, 7K] and Kuan Ch'ung 管崇, a man of Chin-ling 晉陵 [II, 6K] drew together [into their service] 擁 a host of more than a hundred thousand, called themselves Generals [*chiang-chün* 將軍] and raided to the left [east] of the Yangtze [lit. Chiang 江]. [More details in *TCTC*, ch. 182, p. 11a.] . . .

Day 52 [September 3], the bandit leader Ch'ên Tien 陳瑱 and others, a host of thirty thousand, attacked and overthrew Hsin-an-chün 信安郡 [in present Kuangtung]. . . .

9th moon, day 16 [September 27], Wu Hai-liu 吳海流, a man of Chi-yin, and P'êng Hsiao-ts'ai 彭孝才, a man of Tung-hai 東海 [II, 5J], both raised troops to become robbers, a host of several ten thousand.   p. 7a
[Note reference to P'eng Hsiao-ts'ai, Ta-yeh 10th year (614), 12th moon. *TCTC*, ch. 182, p. 16b.]

Day 17 [September 28], the bandit leader Liang Hui-shang 梁慧尚, leading a host of forty thousand, overthrew Ts'ang-wu-chün 蒼梧郡 [in present Kuangtung]. . . .

Day 34 [October 15], Li San-êrh 李三兒 and Hsiang Tan-tzŭ 向但子, men of Tung-yang 東陽 [in present central Chekiang] raised troops and rebelled [lit. caused a disturbance]; [their] host reached more than ten thousand. . . .

10th moon, day 14 [November 24], the bandit leader Lü Ming-hsing 呂明星 led a host of several thousand to besiege Tung-chün 東郡 [II, 4H]. The *hu-pên lang-chiang* 虎賁郎將 [*TCTC*, ch. 182, p. 12a. *Sui-shu* reads *wu* 武 instead of *hu* to avoid T'ang taboo. Li Hu 李虎 ·was the personal name of the grandfather of the first Emperor of the T'ang dynasty, Li Yüan. See *Chiu T'ang-shu*, ch. 1, p. 1a.] Fei Ch'ing-nu 費青奴 attacked and decapitated him. . . .

p. 7b   Day 29 [December 9], . . . Chu Hsieh and Kuan Ch'ung set up Liu Yüan-chin as "emperor". [The Emperor] sent the General T'u Wan-hsü [or T'u-wan Hsü] 吐萬緒 and Yü Chü-lo 魚俱羅 to punish them. Throughout the year and into the next they had not been able to overcome [them]. [These rebels were defeated and killed in 614 by the Sui official Wang Shih-ch'ung 王世充. *Sui-shu*, ch. 70, p. 10a, and *Chiu T'ang-shu*, ch. 54, p. 1b.]   Mêng-Jang 孟讓 and Wang Po 王薄, men of Ch'i 齊 [II, 3I], and others, a host of more than ten thousand held the Ch'ang-pai Mountains [Ch'ang-pai-shan 長白山 I] and swiftly attacked 攻剽 all the commanderies.   Chang Chin-ch'êng 張金稱, the bandit of Ch'ing-ho 清河 [II, 3H], [had] a host of several ten thousand [*Pei-shih* gives 衆各數萬]. Ko Ch'ien 格謙, bandit leader of P'o-hai 渤海 [II, 3I], styled himself King of Yen 燕王 [cf. *TCTC*, ch. 183, p. 9b].   Sun Hsüan-ya 孫宣雅 styled himself King of Ch'i 齊王. [Their] hosts [were] each a hundred thousand.   East of the Mountains was afflicted. . . .

11th moon, day 46 [December 26], the General of the Right Archer Guard [*yu-hou-wei chiang-chün* 右候衛將軍] Fêng Hsiao-tz'ŭ 馮孝慈 attempted to suppress [lit. punished] Chang Chin-ch'êng at Ch'ing-ho, but was defeated by him. [Fêng] Hsiao-tz'ŭ was killed. [Cf. *TCTC*, ch. 182, p. 12b.]

p. 8a   12th moon . . . day 24 [February 2, 614], Hsiang Hai-ming 向海明, a man of Fu-fêng 扶風 [II, 5D] raised troops and rebelled.   He called [himself] "emperor" and established the first [year (i.e. of a new reign title)] of Pai-wu 白烏 [the White Crow]. [The Emperor] sent the President of the Court of Imperial Equipage [*t'ai-p'u-ch'ing* 太僕卿] Yang I-ch'ên 楊義臣 to attack and defeat him. [More details in *TCTC*, ch. 182, pp. 13a–13b.]   [Tu Fu-wei 杜伏威 raided Huai-nan 淮南 (II, 6I).   This and other details concerning him and his associates are entered at this chronological point in *TCTC*, ch. 182, p. 14b.]

p. 9a   [Ta-yeh] 10th year [614], . . . 2nd moon . . . day 34 [April 13].   T'ang Pi 唐弼, a man of Fu-fêng, raised troops in rebellion; [his] host numbered a hundred thousand.   He set up Li Hung 李弘 [*TCTC*, ch. 182, p. 15a, reads Li Hung-chih 李弘芝] as "emperor" and called himself King of T'ang. . . .

4th moon, day 8 [May 17], Chang Ta-hu 張大虎 [*Sui-shu* reads

Ta-piao 大彪 to avoid T'ang taboo. *TCTC*, ch. 182, p. 15a, reads Ta-hu], bandit of P'êng-ch'êng 彭城 [II, 5I], gathered a host of several ten thousand. Having fortified themselves at [lit. guarding] the Hsüan-po Mountains 懸薄山 [location not identified] [they] became robbers. [The Emperor] sent Tung Shun 董純, Commandery Administrator [*t'ai-shou* 太守] of Yü-lin 榆林 [II, 1F] to attack. He defeated and decapitated [the bandit]. [Cf. *TCTC*, ch. 182, p. 15a.] . . .

5th moon . . . day 39 [June 17], the bandit leader Sung Shih-mo 宋世謨 overthrew Lang-yeh-chün 琅邪郡 [II, 4J].   p. 9b

Day 57 [July 5], Liu Chia-lun 劉迦論, a man of Yen-an 延安 [II, 3E], raised troops in rebellion, called himself "imperial king" [*huang-wang* 皇王], and established the first [year] of Ta-shih 大世. [In *TCTC*, ch. 182, p. 15a, this note is followed by an account of his defeat at the hands of the general Ch'ü-t'u T'ung 屈突通.]

6th moon, day 8 [July 16], the bandit leaders Chêng Wên-ya 鄭文雅, Lin Pao-hu 林寶護 and others, a host of thirty thousand, overthrew Chien-an-chün 建安郡 [present Min-hou (Foochow)]. Yang Ching-hsiang 楊景祥, the Commandery Administrator, was killed.

. . . 7th moon, . . . day 1 [September 7]. Koguryŏ [lit. Kao-li 高麗] sent an envoy asking to submit. . . .

[8th moon (September 9-October 8), item concerning bandits stealing (imperial ?) horses, *TCTC*, ch. 182, pp. 15b-16a.]

11th moon, . . . day 46 [December 21], the bandit leader Ssŭ-ma Ch'ang-an 司馬長安 broke into Ch'ang p'ing-chün 長平郡 [II, 4G].

Day 52 [December 27], Liu Miao-wang 劉苗王, a Hu 胡 [northern "barbarian"] of Li-shih 離石 [II, 3F], raised troops in rebellion and called himself "emperor", appointing his younger brother Liu-êrh[3] to be King of Yung-an 永安王. His host reached several ten thousand. The General P'an Ch'ang-wên 潘長文 attempted to suppress him [lit. punished him], [but] could not overcome him.   p. 10a

In this moon [December 7, 614–January 4, 615] the bandit leader [of Chi-chün 汲郡, *TCTC*, ch. 182, p. 16a] Wang Tê-jên 王德仁 drew together [into his service] a host of several ten thousand. Fortifying themselves at [lit. guarding] the Lin-lü Mountains 林廬山, [they] became robbers.

12th moon, . . . day 27 [January 31, 615], the bandit leader Mêng Jang, [with] a host of more than a hundred thousand, took the Tu-liang Palace 都梁宮 [II, 6J]. Wang Shih-ch'ung, Assistant Commandery Administrator [*chün-ch'êng* 郡丞. *Pei-shih* omits the *chün*] of Chiang-tu 江都 [II, 6J], sent [by the Emperor], attacked and defeated him

---

3. The text gives 第六兒 meaning "his sixth son," but this is probably a misprint for 弟.

[i.e. Mêng Jang]. [Wang Shih-ch'ung] captured his entire host. [Mêng Jang himself escaped. See details in *TCTC*, ch. 182, pp. 16b–17a]. [Further notes concerning Lu Ming-yüeh 盧明月, bandit leader of Cho-chün 涿郡 (II, 1H), and other bandits opposed by the official Chang Hsü-t'o 張須陁, are given at the end of this moon in *TCTC*, ch. 182, pp. 17a–17b.]

[Ta-yeh] 11th year [615] . . . 1st moon, . . . day 35 [February 8], the *hu-pên lang-chiang* [*Sui-shu* reads *wu* to avoid T'ang taboo. Cf. above: 9th year, 10th moon, day 14] Kao Chien-p'i 高建毗 defeated the bandit leader Yen Hsüan-chêng 顏宣政 at Ch'i-chün 齊郡 [II, 3I] and took prisoner several thousand men and women. . . .

p. 10b 2nd moon, day 5 [March 10], the bandit leader Yang Chung-hsü 楊仲緒, leading a host of more than ten thousand, attacked Pei-p'ing 北平 [II, 1J]. Li Ching[4] Duke of Hua 滑公, defeated and decapitated him. [*Sui-shu*, ch. 65, pp. 9b–10a, places these events in the next year, 616.] . . .

Day 13 [March 18], Wang Hsü-pa 王須拔, a man of Shang-ku 上谷 [II, 2H], rebelled. He called himself King of Man-t'ien 漫天王. [His] state was styled Yen 燕. The bandit leader Wei Tiao-êrh 魏刁兒 called himself Li-shan-fei 歷山飛. [Their] hosts each [numbered] over a hundred thousand. [To] the north [they] allied themselves with the Turks, [to] the south [they] raided Chao 趙 [northern Shansi. *TCTC*, ch. 182, p. 18a, reads Yen 燕 and Chao, hence including also the northern end of the north China plain]. . . .

5th moon [*Pei-shih* gives 3rd moon (April 4–May 3). According to *TCTC*, ch. 182, pp. 18a–19a, 3rd moon would be correct], day 34 [June 7], they slew [by imperial command] the Generalissimo of the Right Brave Guard [*yu-hsiao-wei ta-chiang-chün* 右驍衞大將軍] *kuang-lu ta-fu* 光祿大夫[5], Duke of Ch'êng 郕公, Li Hun 李渾, and [the Director of] the Administration of Works [*chiang-tso-chien* 將作監] *kuang-lu ta-fu*, Li Min 李敏. Both their families were exterminated.

Day 40 [June 13], the bandit leader Ssŭ-ma Ch'ang-an overran Hsi-ho-chün 西河郡 [II, 3F]. . . .

p. 11a 7th moon, day 36 [August 8], Chang Ch'i-hsü 張起緒, a man of Huai-nan, raised troops as robbers. [His] host reached thirty thousand. . . .

[8th moon, day 10 (September 11) to 9th moon, day 41 (October 12), Emperor Yang was besieged at Yen-mên 鴈門 (II, 2G).]

4. 李景, d. after 618. *CCBN*, p. 425. Biography in *Sui-shu*, ch. 65, and in *Pei-shih*, ch. 76.

5. The modern pronunciation for the phrase 大夫 is *tai-fu*, but it is not known that such a variant from the usual pronunciation of these characters was used in the case of the above title in Sui or T'ang times. *Ta-fu* is used in Chavannes, *Tou-kiue occidentaux*, p. 23.

10th moon, ... day 4 [November 4], Wei Ch'i-lin 魏騏驎, a man of P'êng-ch'êng, collecting a host of more than ten thousand, became a robber and raided Lu-chün 魯郡 [II, 4I].

Day 9 [November 9], the bandit leader Lu Ming-yüeh, collecting a host of more than a hundred thousand, raided between Ch'ên 陳 and Ju 汝 [T'ang prefectures, *chou,* at Huai-yang-chün 淮陽郡 (II, 5H) and Hsiang-ch'êng-chün 襄城郡 (II, 5G) respectively]. Li Tzǔ-t'ung   p. 11b 李子通, bandit leader of Tung-hai 東海 [II, 5J], drawing together [into his service] a host, crossed over the Huai 淮 [River]. He styled himself King of Ch'u 楚王, established the first [year] of Ming-chêng 明政, and raided Chiang-tu. [*TCTC*, ch. 182, p. 22a, gives other details concerning Li Tzǔ-t'ung, including an account of fighting between him and Tu Fu-wei.]

11th moon [see *Pei-shih*; *Sui-shu* reads 12th, by mistake], day 52 [December 22], the bandit leader Wang Hsü-pa overran Kao-yang-chün 高陽郡 [earlier called Po-ling-chün 博陵郡 (II, 2H), present Ting-hsien 定縣].

12th moon, ... day 17 [January 16, 616] [*TCTC*, ch. 182, p. 22b, gives day 27], [the Emperor] ordered the President of the Board of Public Revenues [*min-pu shang-shu* 民部尚書] Fan Tzǔ-kai[6] to lead out troops of the Region within the Passes [Kuan-chung 關中] to punish the bandits of Chiang-chün 絳郡 [II, 4F], Ching P'an-t'o 敬盤陀 and Ch'ai Pao-ch'ang 柴保昌. A year passed without [his] being able to overcome [them]. [See *Sui-shu*, ch. 63, pp. 4b–5a.] Chu Ts'an 朱粲 a man of Ch'iao chün 譙郡 [II, 5H], having drawn together a crowd of several hundred thousand, raided Ching-hsiang 荊襄 [Hsiang-yang-chün 襄陽郡 (II, 6F) in the ancient province of Ching]. He usurped the title Emperor of Ch'u 楚帝 and established the first [year] of Ch'ang-ta 昌達. Most of the commanderies south of the Han 漢 [River] were overthrown by him. [Cf. *TCTC*, ch. 182, pp. 22a–22b, for all the items of this day. Cf. also *Chiu T'ang shu*, ch. 56, p. 13b.]

[Ta-yeh] 12th year [616] ... 1st moon, day 31 [January 30], Ti [or Chai] Sung-po 翟松柏, a man of Yen-mên, raised troops at Ling-ch'iu 靈丘 [II, 2G]. [His] host reaching several ten thousand, he made successive attacks on the neighboring districts [*hsien*]. ...

2nd moon, ... day 60 [February 28], Lu Kung-hsien 盧公暹, bandit of Tung-hai, leading a host of over ten thousand, fortified himself in [lit. guarded at] the Ts'ang Mountains 蒼山 [II, 4J].

4th moon, ... day 60 [April 28], Chên Ti- [or Chai]-êrh 甄翟兒, a   p. 12a subordinate commander under Wei Tao-êrh 魏刀兒所部將 [also

---

6. 樊子蓋, 545–616. *CCBN*, p. 1504. Biography in *Sui-shu*, ch. 63, and in *Pei-shih*, ch. 76.

written Tiao-êrh 刁兒, see above 11th year, 2nd moon, day 13], again [*Pei-shih* omits 復] styled Li-shan-fei 歷山飛,[7] [his] host numbering a hundred thousand, made successive raids on T'ai-yüan 太原 [II, 3G]. General P'an Ch'ang-wên made war against [lit. punished] him, but on the contrary was defeated by him. [P'an] Ch'ang-wên was killed. [Cf. *TCTC*, ch. 183, p. 1b.] . . . .

7th moon, . . . day 1 [August 18], [the Emperor] set out for the Chiang-tu Palace [Chiang-tu kung 江都宮]. . . .

Day 5 [August 31], Sun Hua 孫華 a man of P'ing-i 馮翊 [II, 4E], styled himself Military Commander [*tsung-kuan* 總管], and raised troops to become robbers. Hsi Pao-ch'ê 洗寶徹, *t'ung-shou* 通守 [a commandery official] of Kao-liang 高涼 [in present southern Kuang-tung] raised troops and rebelled [lit. caused a disturbance]. Most of [those dwelling in] ravines or caves of Ling-nan 嶺南 [T'ang province, *tao* 道, in present Kuangtung and Kuangsi][8] were favorable to him. . . .

p. 12b

8th moon, day 42 [October 7], the bandit leader Chao Wan-hai 趙萬海, [his] host [numbering] several hundred thousand, went from Hêng-shan 恒山 [II, 2H] to raid Kao-yang 高陽. . . . .

9th moon, day 34 [October (?); "day 34", *ting-yu* 丁酉, is probably an error], Tu Fu-wei, a man of Tung-hai, and Shên Mi-ti 沈覓敵, of Yang-chou 揚州 [T'ang name for Chiang-tu-chün], and others rebelled [caused a disturbance], [their] host reaching to several ten thousand. Ch'ên Lêng 陳稜, General of the Right Defense Guard [*yu-yü-wei chiang-chün* 右禦衛將軍], attacked and defeated them. . . .

Day 59 [October 24], Li-fei Shih-hsiung 茘非世雄, a man of An-ting 安定 [II, 4D], killed the Magistrate [*ling* 令] of Lin-ching 臨涇 [II, 4D], raised troops and rebelled [lit. caused a disturbance]. He styled himself General [*chiang-chün*].

[10th moon, day 47 (December 11), Li Mi 李密 defeated Chang Hsü-t'o 張須陀, *t'ung-shou* of Jung-yang 榮陽 (II, 5G). *TCTC*, ch. 183, p. 6a. This and many other details concerning Li Mi and Ti (or Chai) Jang 翟讓 are given at this point in *TCTC*, ch. 183, pp. 3b–6b.]

. . . 12th moon, day 20 [January 13, 617], Ts'ao T'ien-ch'êng 操天成 [*TCTC*, ch. 183, p. 6b, reads Ts'ao Shih-ch'i 操師乞 and puts these events just before 12th moon], bandit of P'o-yang 鄱陽 [east of P'o-yang Lake in Kiangsi] raised troops in rebellion, styled himself King of Yüan-hsing 元興王, and established the first [year] of Shih-hsing 始興. He attacked and overthrew Yü-chang-chün 豫章郡 [in Kiangsi], [*TCTC*, ch. 183, pp. 6b–7a, adds details concerning the death of Ts'ao

p. 13a

---

7. It may be that Wei Tao-êrh had died and that the former subordinate uses his title again.

8. This refers possibly to fugitives, but probably to "barbarians".

and concerning his subordinate Lin Shih-hung 林士弘, who succeeded to the command of their forces.] . . .

Day 29 [January 22, 617], Lin Shih-hung, a man of P'o-yang, called himself "emperor", his state was styled Ch'u 楚, and he established the first [year] of T'ai-p'ing 太平. He attacked and overthrew Chiu-chiang 九江 [-chün] and Lu-ling-chün 廬陵郡 [both in Kiangsi]. [*TCTC*, ch. 183, p. 7a, gives further details concerning his territorial limits.] The Duke of T'ang 唐公 [i.e. Li Yüan 李淵] defeated Chên Ti-[or Chai-]êrh at Hsi-ho. He took prisoner several thousand men and women.

[Further details concerning rebels are given at this point in *TCTC*, ch. 183. Chang Chin-ch'êng, Kao Shih-ta 高士達 and others raided Ho-pei 河北, i.e. north of the Yellow River in the north China plain. These two were defeated and killed by the Sui official, Yang I-chên. But one of Kao Shih-ta's adherents, Tou Chien-tê 竇建德 established himself at P'ing-yüan, styled himself General (*chiang-chün*) and collected a following of more than a hundred thousand men (pp. 7a–8b). Another group was active along the seacoast. Ko Ch'ien had seized Tou-tzŭ-kang 豆子航 [II, 3I], but was defeated and killed by the Sui official Wang Shih-ch'ung. His adherent Kao K'ai-tao 高開道 of P'o-hai led the remainder of his host to raid and plunder the region of Yen 燕, i.e. the northern end of the north China plain (p. 9b). Further details concerning disturbed conditions in this region, including revolt of Lo I 羅藝 at Cho-chün (pp. 9b–10a).]

[Li Yüan helped Wang Jên-kung 王仁恭, Commandery Administrator (*t'ai-shou*) of Ma-i, against the Turks. *TCTC*, ch. 183, pp. 10a–10b.]

[Ta-yeh] 13th year [617] . . . 1st moon, day 49 [February 11], Tu Fu-wei, the bandit of Ch'i-chün, leading [his] host across the Huai 淮 [River], attacked and overthrew Li-yang-chün 歷陽郡. [More details in *TCTC*, ch. 183, pp. 10b–11a.]

Day 53 [February 15], Tou Chien-tê, a bandit of P'o-hai, set up an altar for sacrifices at Lo-shou 樂壽 in Ho-chien [-chün] 河間[郡] [II, 2H], called himself King of Ch'ang-lo 長樂王, and established the first [year] of Ting-ch'ou 丁丑.[9] [Cf. *TCTC*, ch. 183, p. 11a.]

Day 18 [March 12], the bandit leader Hsü Yüan-lang,[10] leading a host of several thousand, overran Tung-p'ing-chün 東平郡 [II, 4H]. [More details in *TCTC*, ch. 183, p. 11a.] Tao Hsien-ch'êng 到公成, a man of Hung-hua 弘化 [II, 4D], gathered a host of over ten thousand men to become robbers. The nearby commanderies were afflicted

---

9. These were the cyclical characters for the year Ta-yeh 13th year; *Kang-mu*, ch. 37, p. 61a.

10. 徐圓朗, d. 624. *CCBN*, p. 792. Biography in *Chiu T'ang-shu*, ch. 55, and in *T'ang-shu*, ch. 86 (Tr. Pfizmaier, "Gründung des Thang," pp. 44–46.)

thereby. [Lu Ming-yüeh, having plundered in Ho-nan 河南 (i.e. south of the Yellow River) as far as the north bank of the Huai River, was defeated and killed by Wang Shih-ch'ung at Nan-yang 南陽 II, 6F. *TCTC*, ch. 183, p. 11a.]

2nd moon, day 19 [March 13], Liang Shih-tu 梁師都, a man of Shuo-fang 朔方 [II, 2E], killed the Assistant Commandery Administrator [*chün-ch'eng*], T'ang Shih-tsung 唐世宗, seized the commandery, and rebelling called himself Great Chancellor [*ta-ch'êng-hsiang* 大丞相]. [The Emperor] sent the *yin-ch'ing kuang-lu ta-fu* 銀青光祿大夫 [an honorary title] Chang Shih-lung 張世隆, to attack him, but on the contrary [Chang Shih-lung] was defeated by him. [More details in *TCTC*, ch. 183, p. 11a.]

p. 13b   Day 25 [March 19], the bandit leader Wang Tzŭ-ying 王子英 overran Shang-ku-chün.

Day 26 [March 20], Liu Wu-chou 劉武周, *hsiao-wei* 校尉 of Ma-i, killed the Commandery Administrator [*t'ai-shou*] Wang Jên-kung and raised troops in rebellion [lit. to cause disturbance]. He turned north to join the Turks and called himself Ting-yang Khan 定楊可汗. [This title was conferred on him by Shih-pi Khan after Liu Wu-chou's victories in the next moon. For this and other details, see *TCTC*, ch. 183, pp. 11a–11b and 14a.]

Day 27 [March 21], the bandit leaders Li Mi, Ti Jang, and others overthrew the Hsing-lo Granary [Hsing-lo ts'ang 興洛倉]. [Yang] T'ung 侗, Prince of Yüeh 越王, sent the *hu-pên lang-chiang* [Sui-shu gives *wu* instead of *hu*] Liu Ch'ang-kung 劉長恭 and the Vice President of the Court of Imperial Banquets [*kuang-lu shao-ch'ing* 光祿少卿] Fang Tsê 房則 to attack them, but on the contrary they [i.e. the officials] were defeated by them. The dead [amounted to] five or six out of [every] ten.

Day 37 [March 31], Li Mi styled himself Duke of Wei 魏公 and announced the first year [of a new era]. He opened the granary in order to distribute freely to [his] crowd of partisans [lit. robbers] 振群盜 [*Pei-shih* here reads 賑郡 instead of 振群; *TCTC*, ch. 183, p. 12b, reads 恣民; *Chiu T'ang-shu*, ch. 53, p. 5b, reads 恣人; and *T'ang-shu*, ch. 84, p. 4a, reads 賑食]. [His] host reached several hundred thousand. All the commanderies of South of the [Yellow] River successively were overthrown by him. [Elaboration of these items concerning Li Mi in *TCTC*, ch. 183, pp. 11b–14a.]

Day 39 [April 2], Liu Wu-chou defeated the *hu-pên lang-chiang* [*Sui-shu* gives *wu* instead of *hu*] Wang Chih-pien 王智辯 at Sang-kan-chên 桑乾鎮 [II, 1G]. [Wang] Chih-pien was killed. [More details in *TCTC*, ch. 183, p. 14a.]

3rd moon, day 55 [April 18], Chang Tzŭ-lu 張子路, a man of Lu-chiang 廬江 [II, 6I], raised troops in rebellion. Ch'ên Lêng, General of the Right Defense Guard, having been sent [by the Emperor], suppressed [lit. punished] him and pacified [the people of his locality].

[Day 4 (April 27), Liu Wu-chou overran Lou-fan-chün 樓煩郡 and seized the Fên-yang Palace 汾陽宮. He and Liang Shih-tu were both granted the title of Khan or "emperor" (which here seems to have been one and the same thing) by Shih-pi Khan. Details concerning them and the rebel Kuo Tzŭ-ho 郭子和 of Yü-lin 榆林 (II, 1F) are given at this point in *TCTC*, ch. 183, pp. 14a–14b.]

Day 14 [May 7], the bandit leader Li T'ung-tê 李通德, [his] host [numbering] a hundred thousand, raided Lu-chiang. Chang Chên-chou 張鎮州, General of the Left Garrison Guard [*tso-t'un-wei chiang-chün* 左屯衛將軍] attacked and defeated him.

. . . 4th moon, day 20 [May 13], Hsieh Chü 薛舉, *hsiao-wei* of Chin-ch'êng 金城 [II, 4B], leading a host in rebellion, called himself King Lord Protector of Western Ch'in [Hsi Ch'in *pa-wang* 西秦霸王] and established the first [year] of Ch'in-hsing 秦興. He attacked and overthrew the commanderies of Lung-yu. [More details in *TCTC*, ch. 183, pp. 14b–15a.]

Day 26 [May 19], the bandit leader Mêng Jang entered the outer suburbs of the eastern capital [Lo-yang 洛陽. See Ho-nan-chün 河南郡, II 5G] by night, and withdrew after burning the Fêng-tu Market 豐都市. [Mêng Jang was a subordinate of Li Mi. See *TCTC*, ch. 183, pp. 15a–15b.]

p. 14a

Day 30 [May 23], Li Mi overthrew the Eastern Hui lo Granary [Hui-lo tung-ts'ang 廻洛東倉. Cf. *TCTC*, ch. 183, p. 16a, which reads Hui-lo ts'ang (II, 5G). This item is included among extensive details concerning Li Mi, pp. 15b–17a.]

Day 34 [May 27], the bandit leader Fang Hsien-po 房憲伯 overthrew Ju-yin-chün 汝陰郡 [II, 6H]. [Cf. *TCTC*, ch. 183, p. 16b.]

In this month the *kuang-lu ta-fu* [*Pei-shih* adds *wu-pên lang-chiang* (*wu* used for *hu*)] P'ei Jên-chi 裴仁基 and Chao T'o 趙陀, Commandery Administrator of Huai-yang, both rebelled with their hosts and sided with Li Mi. [Cf. *TCTC*, ch. 183, p. 16b.]

5th moon, day 1 [June 23], the Duke of T'ang raised a "Righteous Army" 義師 at T'ai-yüan.

APPENDIX E

ADDITIONAL UPRISINGS, 617

Rebels and bandits of Ta-yeh 13th year (617) (excluding those already listed in *Appendix D*), translated from the annals of the T'ang dynasty, *T'ang-shu*, ch. 1.

T'ang-shu, At this time [about 617] . . . Shao Chiang-hai 邵江海 seized Ch'i-chou
ch. 1, p. 3a 岐州 [T'ang prefecture, *chou*. Sui: Fu-fêng-chün][1] and styled [himself] King of Hsin-p'ing 新平王.

. . . Wang Hua 汪華 revolted at Hsin-an 新安 [in present southern Anhui] . . . [and] styled [himself] King of Wu 吳王. . . .

Tso Ts'ai-hsiang 左才相 revolted at Ch'i-chün 齊郡 and styled himself Duke of Po-shan 博山. . . .

Tso Nan-tang 左難當 seized Ching 涇 [T'ang prefecture. Sui: An-ting-chün.]

Fêng Yang 馮盎 seized Kao-lo 高羅 [in present Hupei. Sui location not identified.]

All styled [themselves] Military Commanders [*tsung-kuan* 總管]. . . .

Chou Wên-chü 周文舉 seized Huai-yang, and styled [his forces] Liu-yeh-chün 柳葉軍. . . .

Chang Ch'ang-hsün 張長遜 seized Wu-yüan 五原 [II, 1D].

Chou T'ao 周洮 seized Shang-lo 上洛 [II, 5E].

Yang Shih-lin 楊士林 seized Shan-nan 山南 [T'ang province, *tao*, in the Han River valley]. . . .

p. 3b Yang Chung-ta 楊仲達 seized Yü-chou 豫州. [He probably seized part of the ancient province of Yü in central and southern Honan.]

Chang Shan-hsiang 張善相 seized I-ju 伊汝. [Probably to be identified with the Sui commandery, Hsiang-ch'êng-chün. Previously called first I-chou, later Ju-chou. Known also as I-chou, and later as Ju-chou, in T'ang times.]

Wang Yao-han 王要漢 seized Pien-chou 汴州 [Sui: Chün-i 浚儀, II, 5H.]

Shih Tê-jui 時德叡 seized Yü-shih [or Wei-shih] 尉氏 [II, 5G].

Li I-man 李義滿 seized P'ing-ling 平陵 [II, 6F].

Ch'i Kung-shun 綦公順 seized Ch'ing-lai 青萊 [Lai-chou (Sui: Tung-lai-chün 東萊郡, II, 3J) in the ancient province of Ch'ing]

---

1. T'ang place-names are identified according to the Sui names of 617. Characters and map locations are given only if not previously mentioned in Appendix D.

Ch'un Yü-nan 淳于難 seized Wên-têng 文登 [II, 3K].

Hsü Shih-shun 徐師順[2] seized Jên-ch'êng 任城 [II, 4I].

Chiang Hung-tu 蔣弘度 seized Tung-hai. . . .

Chiang Shan-ho 蔣善合 seized Yün-chou 鄆州 [T'ang prefecture. Sui: Hsü-ch'ang 須昌, II, 4I].

T'ien Liu-an 田留安 seized Chang-ch'iu 章丘 [II, 3I].

Chang Ch'ing-t'ê 張青特 seized Chi-pei.

Tsang Chün-hsiang 臧君相 seized Hai-chou 海州 [Sui: Tung-hai-chün].

Yin Kung-sui 殷恭邃 seized Shu-chou 舒州 [Sui: T'ung-an-chün 同安郡, II, 7I].

Chou Fa-ming 周法明 seized Yung-an 永安 [II, 7H].

Miao Hai-ch'ao 苗海潮 seized Yung-chia 永嘉 [in present southern Chekiang].

Mei Chih-yen 梅知巖 seized Hsüan-ch'êng 宣城 [II, 7J].

Têng Wên-chin 鄧文進 seized Li-chiu [or Li-ch'iu] 俚酋 in Kuang-chou廣州 [Sui: Nan-hai-chün 南海郡, the commandery which included the site of modern Canton.]

Yang Shih-lüeh 楊世略 seized Hsün 循 and Ch'ao 潮 [T'ang prefectures. Sui: Lung-ch'uan-chün 龍川郡 and I-an-chün 義安郡 respectively. In present Kuangtung.]

Jan An-ch'ang 冉安昌 seized Pa-tung 巴東 [II, 7E].

Ning Ch'ang-chên 甯長真 seized Yü-lin 鬱林 [in present Kuangsi]. . .

2. Probably Hsü Yüan-lang. See Appendix D, Ta-yeh 13th year (617), 1st moon, day 18, and his biography in *Chiu T'ang-shu*, ch. 55. The latter tells of his conquering all the territory between Lang-yeh-chün and Tung-p'ing-chün (II, 4J and 4H), p. 17a. This would include Jên-ch'êng.

APPENDIX F

DESCRIPTION OF MAPS

Map I is intended to present some idea of the extent of the Sui empire at its height, about 610, including the conquest of the T'u-yü-hun territory and the trade routes which led into Turkistan. Sui armies invaded Koguryŏ (here indicated by its Chinese name, Kao-li) after 610, but civil administration did not extend beyond the Liao River. Map I also indicates the approximate location during the time of Emperor Yang of China's principal neighbors, especially those referred to in the text.

Maps II-A and II-B indicate places in North and Central China referred to in the main chapters of this volume and in Appendices D and E with the nomenclature as used during most of the reign of Emperor Yang, i.e. from 607-618 (see Chapter II, section on "Internal Administration"). Commandery (*chün*) names are entered in their full form, that is with the suffix *-chün*, e.g. Pei-p'ing-chün. District (*hsien*) names are given without a special ending, e.g. Hua-yin. In some cases two names appear opposite one locality, the name of the commandery and the name of its administrative center. For example, T'ai-yüan-chün was administered from the district city of Chin-yang.

Map II-A is intended to show the location of uprisings in north and central China from Ta-yeh 9th year (613) up to Ta-yeh 13th (617), 5th moon, the latter being the date of Li Yüan's revolt in T'ai-yüan. Aside from those commanderies which are mentioned in the sources as scenes of revolt, only some of the other more important ones have been included.

The red numbers 9, 10, 11, 12 and 13 refer to years of the Ta-yeh reign period (605-617), corresponding roughly to 613, 614, 615, 616, and 617 respectively (see Appendix A). The number (13), in parenthesis, indicates outbreaks dated only in *T'ang-shu*, ch. 1, pp. 3a-3b. (See p. 61 and Appendix E.)

Since it has not been possible to include on Map II-A the locations of rebellions occurring along part of the Yangtze and in south China, the names of commanderies where such uprisings took place are included on Map I.

Map II-B indicates the chief rebels of north and Central China, with their approximate location in 617. It must be remembered that two other rebels controlled large territories south of the region included here. These were Hsiao Hsien on the Central Yangtze (see p. 105) and Lin

142

Shih-hung in what is now Kiangsi (see p. 63). Map II-B also gives the approximate route followed by Li Yüan, Duke of T'ang, in his campaign from T'ai-yüan to the western capital in Ta-yeh 13th year (617), from the 7th moon to the 11th moon (see Chapter X).

The works used in making the maps are discussed in the Bibliography, section on "Geography".

BIBLIOGRAPHY

The following list contains the most important works which have been used in writing this volume as well as a few books and articles which deserve special mention because of their connection with the topic, even though they have not been found useful for this research. As a bibliography it is exclusive, rather than inclusive.

There are other important works in Chinese, Japanese, and western languages which deal with this section of Chinese history and which bear on the founding of the T'ang dynasty. Many of these are well known to the author and are being used in further study of this general subject. The present list contains only those works which are of basic importance in a preliminary survey limited to a study of the disintegration of the Sui empire and the rise of the Li family to preëminence among the various contenders. A comprehensive study of the whole range of Chinese writings which deal with the founding of the T'ang dynasty is in preparation and will be included in a subsequent volume. Such a study will include detailed bibliographical criticism of each item and an evaluation of its place in relation to other works covering the same field. Any attempt to provide such detailed comparisons before more extended research has been completed would be of little or no real value to those who seek an understanding of this literature.

The descriptive comments which supplement the following list are presented merely as brief guides to indicate the reasons for including these works in the Bibliography and to show their importance for this research.

The arrangement has been planned as a means of presenting as clearly as possible the different types of material used in this particular study. The first section indicates how the various items were gathered, the second identifies the Chinese sources on which the research was based, and the third lists a few special studies which contain previous translations from these sources and which are of importance for this particular topic. The last two sections contain other books and articles subdivided according to the manner in which they have contributed towards a study of the sources. The first three subdivisions include important survey volumes covering a wide range of history and the last four contain special studies, important books of reference, and a number of items which might have been differently classified but whose chief importance in this work has been their use as aids in the geographical problems involved.

145

I. Bibliographical Aids

The gathering of bibliographical information for studies in Chinese history has recently been made easier through the excellent catalogues and reference service in a number of libraries of Far Eastern literature in this country. In compiling the present list, the author personally visited the Chinese libraries at the University of California, Harvard University, the Library of Congress, and the National Library in Peiping, China. For Chinese and western works on the early seventh century, a careful search was made through a number of standard bibliographies, among which those listed below were found to be the most important. In addition, files of scholarly reviews dealing with sinology in Chinese and western languages were examined for possible items of importance.

The most valuable work for starting any research on T'ang history is the detailed critical bibliography in the monograph on the T'ang examination system by Robert Des Rotours, *No. 45* in this Bibliography.

1. Chi Yün 紀昀 and others (compilers): *Ssŭ-k'u ch'üan-shu tsung-mu* 四庫全書總目. (Completed 1790. Ta-tung shu-chü 大東書局, 2nd edition, Shanghai, 1930.)

   The great descriptive and critical bibliography of Chinese literature compiled in the reign of Ch'ien-lung, it contains scholarly descriptions of the sources used in this study. See *No. 5*, pp. 22–26, for detailed bibliographical information.

2. Cordier, Henri: *Bibliotheca Sinica. Dictionnaire bibliographique des ouvrages relatifs à l'empire chinois.* (2nd edition, with *Supplément*; Paris, 1904–1924.)

   The standard bibliography of works in European languages.

3. Gardner, Charles Sidney: *A Union List of Selected Chinese Books in American Libraries.* (Washington, 1932.)

   "Principal monuments in all major fields" of Chinese literature. Most items include a brief description in English.

4. Maspero, Henri: "Chine et Asie Centrale" in *Histoire et Historiens depuis cinquante ans: Méthodes, Organisation et Résultats du Travail Historique de 1876, à 1926,* Bibliothèque de la Revue Historique (Paris, 1928), pp. 517–559.

   More recent than *No. 2*, especially valuable as a basis for historical research.

5. Têng Ssŭ-yü and Knight Biggerstaff: *An Annotated Bibliography of Selected Chinese Reference Works*, Yenching Journal of Chinese Studies, Monograph No. 12. (Peiping, 1936.)

A critical guide to the most important Chinese reference works. An invaluable tool for all students of Chinese history.

6. Wieger, Léon: *La Chine à travers les âges, hommes et choses: Index bibliographique.* (Hsien hsien, 1920.)

Based on the Chinese bibliography *Shu-mu ta-wên.* For the latter, see *No. 5*, pp. 2–3.

7. Wylie, Alexander: *Notes on Chinese Literature: with Introductory Remarks on the Progressive Advancement of the Art; and a list of translations from the Chinese into various European languages.* (Reprinted from the original edition of 1867; Shanghai, 1922.)

The most comprehensive western descriptive bibliography of Chinese works. Needs revision.

II. THE CHINESE SOURCES

The early use of paper in China and the damp climate which prevails in most of the country for a large part of every year have resulted in a scarcity of manuscript remains from the time of the Sui or T'ang dynasties. The governmental archives of these periods have long since disappeared. Stone inscriptions have survived and have been carefully recorded in collections which are available in our libraries. As such they form a significant part of the chief sources at our disposal, the printed literature which is based on the writings of the Sui, T'ang, and Sung periods.

Among these writings the most important for a basic understanding of historical events are the so-called "dynastic histories." In the seventh century, as in earlier and later periods, Chinese scholars kept careful written accounts of the events of their time. Historical records were compiled according to traditional forms established centuries before and these were used in the writing of official standard histories. The actual process of compilation has been well described in a recent monograph by Professor Charles S. Gardner of Harvard University. See *No. 56, passim*, especially pp. 86–105.

The following list of sources used in this study includes four dynastic histories, two works (*Nos. 12* and *13*) which were probably used in compiling the T'ang histories, and a general history largely, but not entirely, based on the dynastic histories. In addition, there are included two Chinese works of comment and résumé based on the above.

8. ´Wei Chêng 魏徵, Ch'ang-sun Wu-chi 長孫無忌, and others: *Sui-shu* 隋書. (629–656. Photo-lithographic reprint of the Ch'ien-lung "palace edition" of 1739, T'ung-wên chü of Wu-chou 五洲同文局, 1903.)

Official dynastic history written under the patronage of T'ang T'ai-tsung (Li Shih-min) within fifty years after the events. The official T'ang historians, who were responsible for this history, were men who themselves had turned against the last Sui ruler, Emperor Yang, and parts of their writing are obviously biased against him. This work contains basic annals, monographs, biographies and accounts of foreign countries. In spite of limitations, it is the most reliable record of the events which took place at the end of the Sui dynasty. See also comments in the main text, especially end of Chapter I. Bibliographical information in *No. 1*, ch. XLV, pp. 12a–12b.

9. Li Yen-shou 李延壽, and others: *Pei-shih* 北史. (Completed ca. 644. Photo-lithographic reprint of the Ch'ien-lung "palace edition" of 1739, T'ung-wên shu-chü of Shanghai 上海同文書局, 1894.)

Official history of the Northern Dynasties: Wei, Ch'i, Chou, and Sui; written under the patronage of T'ang T'ai-tsung. Contains basic annals from 386 to 618, biographies and accounts of foreign countries. It is based on the separate dynastic histories of those dynasties, the Sui annals, for example, being an abbreviation and slight modification of those in the *Sui-shu*, (*No. 8*).

10. Liu Hsü 劉昫, and others: *Chiu T'ang-shu* 舊唐書. (945. Photo-lithographic reprint of the Ch'ien-lung "palace edition" of 1739; T'ung-wên shu-chü of Shanghai 上海同文書局, 1884.)

Official dynastic history based on the records of the dynasty and earlier histories of parts of the dynasty. Contains basic annals, monographs, biographies and accounts of foreign countries. From the historical point of view, the text of this history is considered preferable to that of *No. 11* except for the monographs and tables of the latter. See *No. 45*, pp. 57–71, for detailed bibliographical information.

11. Ou-yang Hsiu 歐陽修, Sung Ch'i 宋祁, and others: *T'ang-shu* 唐書 (or *Hsin T'ang-shu* 新唐書). (1060. Photo-lithographic reprint of the Ch'ien-lung "palace edition" of 1739; T'ung-wên shu-chü of Shanghai 上海同文書局, 1884.)

Official dynastic history; stylistic revision of *No. 10* with the addition of material from other writings. Contains basic annals, monographs, tables, biographies and accounts of foreign countries. See *No. 45*, pp. 56–64, for detailed bibliographical information.

12. Wên Ta-ya 溫大雅: *Ta T'ang ch'uang-yeh ch'i-chü-chu* 大唐創業起居注. (618–626. Vol. III in *Ou-hsiang ling-shih* 藕香零拾, compiled by Miao Ch'üan-sun 繆荃孫, 1910.)

A chronological narrative of events concerning Li Yüan and the founding of the T'ang dynasty from 615 up to the proclamation of the dynasty, by an official recorder at Li Yüan's headquarters. See *No. 42*. This narrative differs in many important details from those of the standard dynastic histories. In *No. 1*, ch. XLVII, p. 3a–3b, Wên Ta-ya's work is included among reliable histories, but some doubt is expressed as to whether it gives a true record of events. Many Chinese scholars of the present day consider the book of great importance for the history of this time and deserving of further research. See *No. 42* for additional bibliographical information.

13. Tu Yu 杜佑: *T'ung-tien* 通典. (801. Wu-ying-tien 武英殿 edition, Canton, 1871.)

A study of Chinese institutions from their origins down to ca. 800, especially valuable for the checking of statements in the dynastic histories. See *No. 45*, pp. 84–85, for detailed bibliographical information.

14. Ssŭ-ma Kuang 司馬光: *Tzŭ-chih t'ung-chien* 資治通鑑. (1086. Photo-lithographic reprint of the 1132 reprint; Vols. XCIX–CLXXVIII in *Ssŭ-pu ts'ung-k'an* 四部叢刊, Shanghai, 1922.)

General history of China covering the period from 403 B.C. to A.D. 959 by an outstanding Sung scholar. For the present study this history appears to be based largely on *No. 10*, but all the material is re-arranged chronologically and the style is simpler to read. See *No. 45*, pp. 71–84, for detailed bibliographical information.

15. Chu Hsi 朱熹 and others: *Tzŭ-chih t'ung-chien kang-mu* 資治通鑑綱目. (About 1190. Published with commentaries by later writers; Shan-tung shu-chü 山東書局, 1879.)

Chronological résumé of much of the material in *No. 14* listed under main headings. See *No. 7*, pp. 25–26.

16. Lo Shih-lin 羅士琳, and others: *Chiu T'ang-shu chiao-k'an-chi* 舊唐書校勘記. (1st edition 1846; edition of Chü-ying chai 懼盈齋, 1872, being a supplement to an edition of the *Chiu T'ang-shu*.)

Comparison of various editions of *No. 10* with one another and with citations from other works. Indispensable as an aid to translation of passages from that history. See *No. 45*, p. 118.

III. Translations from the Chinese Sources

A few western monographs contain extensive translations based on the sources described above. Of these translations some have only an indirect value for the present topic and in such cases the monographs have been listed in the section on special studies (see V). Of the others only two (*Nos. 27* and *28*) can be considered thoroughly reliable and they deal primarily with subjects only partially connected with the present topic. *Nos. 17–26* represent the labors of pioneers in Chinese studies. Their translations are of some help but must be checked at every point and used only with great caution.

17. Julien, Stanislas: "Documents historiques sur les Tou-kioue (Turcs), extrait du *Pien-i-tien*, et traduits du chinois." *Journal Asiatique,* Series 6, Vol. III, pp. 325–367, 490–549; and Vol. IV, pp. 200–242, 391–430, 453–477 (Paris, 1864).

Based on a collection of extracts from the dynastic histories. Translation unreliable; but useful as a general survey of Chinese and Eastern Turk relations.

18. Pfizmaier, August: "Lebensbeschreibungen von Heerführern und Würdenträgern des Hauses Sui," *Denkschriften der kaiserlichen Akademie der Wissenschaften. Philosophisch-historische Classe,* Vol. XXXII (Vienna, 1882), pp. 281–377.

————, ————: Eight articles in *Sitzungsberichte der kaiserlichen Akademie der Wissenschaften. Philosophisch-historische Classe* (Vienna):

19.   "Darlegungen aus der Geschichte des Hauses Sui." Vol. XCVII (1881), pp. 627–706.

20.   "Die fremdländischen Reiche zu den Zeiten des Hauses Sui." Vol. XCVII (1881), pp. 411–490.

21.   "Die letzten Zeiten des Reiches der Tsch'in." Vol. XCVIII (1881), pp. 718–751.

22.   "Fortsetzungen aus der Geschichte des Hauses Sui." Vol. CI (1882), pp. 187–266.

23.   "Nachrichten von den alten Bewohnern des heutigen Corea." Vol. LVII (1868), pp. 461–523.

24.   "Seltsamkeiten aus den Zeiten der Thang." Vol. XCIV

(1879), pp. 7–86, and Vol. XCVI (1880) "Seltsamkeiten und Unglück aus den Zeiten der Thang. II," pp. 293–366.

25. "Zur Geschichte der Aufstände gegen das Haus Sui." Vol. LXXXVIII (1878), pp. 729–806.

26. "Zur Geschichte der Gründung des Hauses Thang." Vol. XCI (1878), pp. 21–100.

These translations, *Nos. 18 to 26*, are from the dynastic histories, but are not very accurate; they are given mostly without any critical notes and should only be used together with careful checking in the sources. They are helpful for a cursory reading of the biographies and other materials included in them and have proved valuable as an aid to writing this book.

27. Chavannes, Edouard: *Documents sur les Tou-kiue (Turcs) occidentaux.* No. VI in SBORNIK TRUDOV ORKHONSKOI EKSPEDITSII. (St. Petersburg 1903. A supplement to the errata is in *T'oung Pao*, Ser. II, Vol. V (1904), p. 110, at the end of "Notes additionelles sur les Tou-kiue (Turcs) occidentaux.")

The most valuable and most reliable translation of Chinese source materials for this period.

28. Jäger, Fritz: "Leben und Werk des P'ei Kü. Ein Kapitel aus der chinesischen Kolonialgeschichte," *Ostasiatische Zeitschrift*, Vol. IX (Berlin, 1020–22), pp. 81–115, 216–231.

Careful translations from *No. 8*, dealing mostly with the early reign of Emperor Yang.

IV. HISTORICAL SURVEYS

(a) *Asia and the Far East*

29. d'Herbelot de Molainville, Barthélemy: *Bibliothèque Orientale, ou Dictionnaire Universel Contenant Tout ce qui fait connoître les Peuples de l'Orient. Leurs Histoires et Traditions tant Fabuleuses que Véritables. Leurs Gouvernemens, Politique, Loix, Moeurs, Coûtumes, et les Revolutions de Leurs Empires. Les Arts et Les Sciences, La Theologie, Médecine, Mythologie, Magie, Physique, Morale, Mathematiques, Histoire Naturelle, Chronologie, Géographie, Observations Astronomiques, Grammaire et Réthorique. Les Vies de leurs Saints, Philosophes, Docteurs, Poëtes, Historiens, Captaines, & de tous ceux qui se sont rendus illustres par leur Vertu, leur Sçavoir ou leurs Actions. Des Jugemens Critiques et des Extraits de Leurs Livres. Ecrits en Arabe, Persan ou Turc sur toutes sortes de Matieres & de Professions.* Continuation by Claude Visdelou, and others (La Haye, 1777–1782.)

The "Continuation" by Visdelou contains a brief account of the founding of the T'ang dynasty and as such was especially recommended to the author by the late Dr. Berthold Laufer.

30. Krause, Friedrich E. A.: *Geschichte Ostasiens.*   (Gottingen, 1925.)

    A good secondary account.

31. Grousset, René: *Histoire de l'Extrême-Orient.*   (Paris, 1929.)

    Brief but excellent outline; based on the best European scholarship.   Especially good for foreign relations.   Includes one of the best available western maps of China in Sui and T'ang times.

32. Steiger, George Nye: *A History of the Far East.*   (Boston, 1936.)

    A comprehensive survey, excellent for its general perspective and clear outline of events.   Contains some inaccuracies concerning the events of this period.

(b) China, History and Culture

33. *Ku-chin t'u-shu chi-ch'êng* 古今圖書集成.   (Commenced in the K'ang-hsi period, completed 1726.)

    The great Ch'ing dynasty encyclopedia.   Contains excerpts from *No. 12* as well as from the dynastic histories, etc.   See Lionel Giles, *An Alphabetical Index to the Chinese Encyclopedia*, (London, 1911).   For details concerning editions and contents see *No. 5*, pp. 107–109.

34. *Mémoires concernant l'Histoire, les Sciences, les Arts, les Moeurs, les Usages, etc. des Chinois, par les Missionaires de Pe-kin.*   (Paris, 1776–1814.)

    These memoirs were written by Jesuits living at the Manchu court in the eighteenth century.   Two sections deal directly with the subject of this book.   Amiot, "Suite des Vies ou Portraits des célèbres Chinois" (in Vol. V) contains biographies of men of the T'ang dynasty.   Antoine Gaubil, "Abrégé de l'histoire de la grande dynastie Tang" (in Vols. XV and XVI) is thus defined in the work itself: "Ce qui est dit dans cet abrégé est tiré d'un grand recueil des historiens des dynasties, appelé Nyen-y-sse ou Nyen-y-che, de l'histoire chinoise de Ssema-kouang [*No. 14*], de l'histoire appelée Tong-Kien-Kang-Mou [*No. 15*] et de celle qui est intitulée Li-tay-ki-che-nien-piao."   Vol. XV, p. 399. Neither of these accounts are as useful as *No. 35*.

35. de Mailla, Joseph-Anne-Marie de Moyriac: *Histoire générale de la Chine, ou Annales de cet Empire; traduites du Tong-Kien-Kang-Mou.*   (Paris, 1777–1785.)

Another monumental work of a French Jesuit in Peking. Translated largely from a Manchu version of Chu Hsi's résumé (*No. 15*), this work gives the fullest account of the period in any western language.

36. Cordier, Henri: *Histoire générale de la Chine et de ses relations avec les Pays étrangers depuis les temps les plus anciens jusqu'à la chute de la Dynastie Manchoue.* (Paris, 1920.)

   A useful survey of the more important events of this period, based largely on *No. 35*.

37. Wieger, Léon: *Textes Historiques, Histoire politique de la Chine depuis l'origine, jusqu'en 1912.* (2nd edition, Hsien hsien, 1923.)

   Excerpts from old Chinese histories, supplemented by a free paraphrase in French together with many side remarks. The point of view is that of the orthodox Chinese scholar plus the bias of an unsympathetic French Jesuit.

38. Wilhelm, Richard: *Geschichte der chinesischen Kultur.* (Munich' 1928.) English edition: *A Short History of Chinese Civilization*. Tr. by Joan Joshua. (New York, 1929.)

   Excellent survey of Chinese cultural history up to the Sung period; especially valuable as a background for the present study, it contains only a cursory mention of the fall of the Sui and the rise of the T'ang.

39. Latourette, Kenneth Scott: *The Chinese: Their History and Culture.* (New York, 1934.)

   A careful and thorough outline, the best treatment of its subject in English. Contains excellent bibliographies at the end of each chapter.

(c) *China, Special Histories*

40. Chi Ch'ao-ting: *Key Economic Areas in Chinese History as Revealed in the Development of Public Works for Water-Control.* (London, 1936.)

   This work has been found most useful for its clear explanation of the state economic planning of the Sui period.

41. Shryock, John Knight: *The Origin and Development of the State Cult of Confucius: an Introductory Study.* (New York, 1932.)

   Important for an understanding of Chinese state education and ideology, a field of study mostly outside the range of the present work. It contains references to the administration of Emperor Yang.

V. Special Studies

(a) Sui-T'ang Period

This heading includes a few books and articles restricted to some phase of the Sui-T'ang period. For the same subject see also *Nos. 17* to *28*, listed above as "Translations from the Chinese Sources." Only those works are listed here which are directly connected with the topic of this study. The periodical articles are all by modern scholars who have done special research in the fields of study covered by these articles.

42. Bingham, Woodbridge: "Wên Ta-ya: The First Recorder of T'ang History," *Journal of the American Oriental Society*, Vol. LVII, No. 4 (December, 1937), pp. 368–374.

    Biography (from *No. 10*) of the author of *No. 12*, translation and notes.

43. Boodberg, Peter A.: "Marginalia to the Histories of the Northern Dynasties," *Harvard Journal of Asiatic Studies*, Vol. III, Nos. 3 and 4 (December, 1938), pp. 223–253; and Vol. IV, Nos. 3 and 4 (December, 1939), pp. 230–283.

    The first and fifth sections of these notes include research on the history of the Sui. Especially valuable for this period are "The Rise and Fall of the House of Yang" and "The Family of Yang Chung" (Vol. IV, pp. 253–270, 282–283).

44. Des Rotours, Robert: "Les grands fonctionnaires des provinces en Chine sous la dynastie des T'ang," *T'oung Pao*, 2nd series, Vol. XXV (1927), pp. 219–332.

    This article and *No. 45* have been found most useful as guides to the translation of official titles of the Sui-T'ang period.

45. Des Rotours, Robert: *Le Traité des Examens traduit de la Nouvelle Histoire des T'ang (Chap. XLIV, XLV)*, Bibliothèque de l'Institut des Hautes Etudes Chinoises, Vol. II. (Paris, 1932.)

    The best western monograph on this period. Includes an excellent outline of T'ang government and a sixty-eight page bibliography of Chinese source materials with detailed comments on each work.

46. Ferguson, John C.: "The Six Horses at the Tomb of the Emperor T'ai Tsung of the T'ang Dynasty." *Eastern Art*, Vol. III (1931), pp. 61–71.

Contains information concerning the rivals of the Li family in their struggle for control of China. Recent articles, which Dr. Ferguson and others have written since 1931, present more accurate information on the horses at the tomb of T'ang T'ai-tsung.

47. Fitzgerald, Charles Patrick: *Son of Heaven, A Biography of Li Shih-Min, founder of the T'ang Dynasty.* (Cambridge, England, 1933.)

This work is the first readable English account of the early years of the T'ang dynasty. On the other hand, it cannot be compared with the scholarly monographs of Chavannes (*No. 27*), Jäger (*No. 28*), and Des Rotours (*Nos. 44* and *45*). It contains free paraphrase rather than translation, is based almost entirely on an uncritical use of *No. 14*, and has been found rather inaccurate for the first decades of the seventh century. See reviews by Woodbridge Bingham in *The Pacific Historical Review*, Vol. III, No. 2 (June 1934), pp. 234–237, and in *The Chinese Social and Political Science Review*, Vol. XVIII, No. 3 (October, 1934), pp. 393–412.

48. Maspero, Henri: "Le Protectorat Général d'Annam sous les T'ang. Essai de Géographie Historique." *BEFEO*, Vol. X (1910), pp. 539–584, and 665–682.

49. Sirén, Osvald: "Tch'ang-ngan au temps des Souei et des T'ang." *Revue des Arts Asiatiques*, Vol. IV (Paris, 1927), pp. 40–46, and 98–104.

50. Siu Siang-tch'ou: *L'oeuvre de T'ang T'ai-tsong: Thèse pour le doctorat en droit. Université l'Aurore.* (Shanghai, 1924.)

A general account in Chinese, with French translation; based on *No. 14*, but without critical notes or references to other sources.

(b) Border Regions of China

The following items contain information bearing specifically upon China's neighbors during the Sui-T'ang transition period. A few more which deal with the border regions are included in the final section on "Geography".

51. Cahun, Léon: *Introduction à l'histoire de l'Asie: Turcs et Mongols, des origines à 1405.* (Paris, 1896.)

Not as reliable or as comprehensive as Parker (*No. 54*) for the period of this book.

52. Huang Wên-pi 黃文弼: *Kao-ch'ang* 高昌. (Peiping, 1931.)

Research on Turfan by a modern specialist.

53. Lo Chên- ü: "Kao-ch'ang Ch'ü shih nien-piao" 高昌麴氏年表, *Liao ch*ʸ *tsa chu* 遼居雜著 [*Miscellaneous Writings in Liao*], *I pien* 乙ʸ [*Part II*], (1933.)

    Research by a distinguished Chinese scholar on the chronology of the rulers of Kao-ch'ang (Turfan).

54. Parker, Edward Harper: *A Thousand Years of the Tartars.* (2nd edition, revised; London, 1924.)

    Most comprehensive English account of China's western and northern neighbors. No references to sources.

55. Ross, E. Denison: "The Orkhon Inscriptions. Being a Translation of Professor Vilhelm Thomsen's final Danish rendering," *Bulletin of the School of Oriental Studies, London Institution*, Vol. V (1928–30), Part 4 (London, 1930).

    The two monuments were erected in 732 and 735 with inscriptions in "Runic" (Turkish) and Chinese. This translation is from a new Danish translation of 1922. The inscriptions include comments on Chinese intrigue as used against the Eastern Turks, but do not bear directly on the subject of this study.

(c) Historiography

56. Gardner, Charles Sidney: *Chinese Traditional Historiography.* (Cambridge, 1938.)

    A scholarly and readable monograph, the only work of its kind.

(d) Chronology

57. Hoang, Pierre: *Concordance des Chronologies Néoméniques Chinoise et Européenne.* Variétés Sinologiques No. 29. (Shanghai, 1910.)

    The standard western work for converting Chinese dates into the equivalent western forms, and vice versa.

58. Tchang, Mathias: *Synchronismes Chinois: Chronologie Complète et Concordance avec L'Ere Chrétienne de toutes les dates concernant l'histoire de l'Extrême-Orient (Chine, Japon, Corée, Annam, Mongolie, etc.) (2357 av. J.-C.—1904 apr. J.-C.)* Variétés Sinologiques No. 24. (Shanghai, 1905.)

(e) Biography

59. Allan, C. Wilfrid: *The Makers of Cathay.* (Shanghai, 1909; 2nd edition, Shanghai, 1925.)

   Brief superficial biographies, including one of T'ang T'ai-tsung.

60. Fang I 方毅 and others (compilers): *Chung-kuo jên-ming ta-tz'ŭ-tien* 中國人名大辭典: *Cyclopedia of Chinese Biographical Names.* (7th edition; Shanghai, 1930.)

   The standard Chinese biographical dictionary. No dates are given for most of the men included. See *No. 5*, pp. 203–204, for bibliographical information.

61. Giles, Herbert A.: *A Chinese Biographical Dictionary.* (London and Shanghai, 1898.)

   The best biographical dictionary in a western language. Some dates inaccurate.

(f) Geography

The locations of Sui geographical names have been identified largely by the use of three Chinese works: the "Monograph on Geography" (*Ti-li chih* 地理志) in the *Sui History* (*No. 8*, chs. 29–31), and two standard reference works listed below (*Nos. 64* and *65*). Two important atlases (*Nos. 63* and *72*) had not yet been published when the outline maps were made, but they have subsequently proved useful in checking data already entered. The works of Chavannes (*No. 27*), Grousset (*No. 31*), and Jäger (*No. 28*), and all of the following items were used in making the maps. The titles below have been entered primarily because of the geographical information they contain. The list is divided according to languages of publication, Chinese, Japanese, and European, in that order.

62. Ku Tsu-yü 顧祖禹: *Tu-shih fang-yü chi-yao* 讀史方輿紀要. (1659–1678. Shanghai, 1899.)

   A record of Chinese geographical changes down to the seventeenth century. Modern Japanese index, *No. 66*. See Arthur W. Hummel, *The Library of Congress: Orientalia Added 1933–1934* (Washington, 1935), p. 9, for bibliographical information.

63. Ting Wên-chiang 丁文江, Wêng Wên-hao 翁文灝, Tsêng Shih-ying 曾世英, and others: *Chung-hua min-kuo hsin ti-t'u* 中華民國新

地圖, *Shên-pao liu-shih chou-nien chi-nien* 申報六十周年紀念 (Shanghai, 1934.)

Excellent atlas of China, including regions formerly within the empire. Contains two sets of large-scale maps of China proper and Manchuria, one relief and one political (many old names included as well as modern Republican names), also many special maps.

64. Tsang Li-ho 臧勵龢, and others: *Chung-kuo ku-chin ti-ming ta-tz'ŭ-tien* 中國古今地名大辭典. (Shanghai, 1933.)

Dictionary of ancient and modern Chinese geographical names. Contains fuller and more detailed information than can be found in the geographical references of the *Tz'ŭ-yüan*. Former locations of towns can be determined more accurately than from *No. 65*.

65. Yang Shou-ching 楊守敬: *Li-tai yü-ti-t'u* 歷代輿地圖. (Edition of Yang shih Kuan-hai-t'ang 楊氏觀海堂; completed 1911.)

The best Chinese historical atlas, by an outstanding scholar and geographer of the last years of the Ch'ing dynasty. The large scale maps give invaluable aid for the study of any period preceding the Ch'ing. In the Sui volume, *Sui ti-li chih-t'u* 隋地理志圖, names are given as they were employed in the latter part of the dynasty, i.e. 607–618.

66. Aoyama Sadao 青山定男: *Shina rekidai chimei yōran; dokushi hō yo kiyō sakuyin* 支那歷代地名要覽: 讀史方輿紀要索引. (Institute of Oriental Studies, Tōhō bunka gakuin 東方文化學院, Tokyo, 1933.)   Index to *No. 62*.

67. Aoyama Sadao 青山定男: "Tō-Sō Henga kō 唐宋汴河考: Study on the Canal Pien (汴河) in the Period T'ang and Sung," *Tôhô Gakuhô* 東方學報. Tokyo, No. 2 (December, 1931), pp. 1–49.

68. Yanai Watari 箭內亙: *Tōyō dokushi chizu* 東洋讀史地圖. (Tokyo, 1926.)

ʻJapanese historical atlas. Useful for the regions surrounding China, especially Korea.

69. Chavannes, Edouard: "Les deux plus anciens spécimens de la cartographie chinoise." *Bulletin de l'École française d'Extrême-Orient*, Vol. III (1903), pp. 214–247.

Contains reproductions, translation and critical comment based on two maps of the Sung period.

70. Cressey, George B.: *China's Geographic Foundations: A Survey of the Land and Its People.* (New York, 1934.)

    The best work of its kind in English.

71. Herrmann, Albert: "Die ältesten chinesischen Karten von Zentral- und Westasien," *Ostasiatische Zeitschrift*, Vol. III (1919–1920), pp. 185–198.

    Contains discussion of Central Asiatic geography in the Sui period.

72. Herrmann, Albert: *Historical and Commercial Atlas of China*, Harvard-Yenching Institute Monograph Series, Vol. I. (Cambridge, 1935.)

    A pioneer study of first importance, an indispensable tool for students in all periods of Chinese history. In this atlas (pp. 39–40) the route of the Sui Grand Canal (Pien-ho) does not accord with the conclusions of Aoyama Sadao (*No. 67*).

73. Japanese Government Railways: *Guide to China: with land and sea routes between the American and European continents.* Official Series, Vol. D. (2nd, revised, edition; Tokyo, 1924.)

    Contains useful map of China with detailed relief features.

74. Lattimore, Owen: *The Desert Road to Turkestan.* (Boston, 1929.)

75. National Geographic Society: *Asia and Adjacent Regions*, a special map supplement published with *The National Geographic Magazine*, Vol. LXIV, No. 6 (December, 1933).

76. Playfair, George M. H.: *The Cities and Towns of China: A Geographical Dictionary.* (2nd edition, Shanghai, 1910.)

77. Richard, Louis: *Comprehensive Geography of the Chinese Empire and Dependencies.* Tr. by M. Kennelly. (Shanghai, 1908.)

78. Stanford, Edward, for the China Inland Mission: *Atlas of the Chinese Empire containing separate maps of the eighteen provinces of China proper on the scale of 1:3,000,000 and of the four great dependencies on the scale of 1:7,500,000 together with an index to all the names on the maps and a list of all Protestant mission stations, etc.* (London, 1908.)

79. Stein, Aurel: *On Ancient Central-Asian Tracks: Brief Narrative of Three Expeditions in Innermost Asia and North-Western China.* (London, 1933.)

    Contains excellent map of Chinese Turkistan showing ancient trade routes.

INDEX

Entries in bold-faced type refer to pages where Chinese characters may be found and names identified. Numerals and letters immediately following placenames indicate map references.

Abbreviations, xiv, 1 n. 1

Academy, Administration of the Imperial, (*kuo-tzŭ-chien*), **128**

A-chiu bandit, **130**

Administration, Sui system of, 11, 127–129; reorganization of, 11, 12; education connected with, 12; extent of, 26, 37, 142; new territory, 29; T'ang organization of, 108, 109, 111. *See also* Government, State, Sui

Administrations (*chien*), **128, 129**

Administrator, *see* Commandery Administrator

Afghanistan, 36 n. 24

Agate goblets, 26

Agricultural Control, Court of, (*ssŭ-nung-ssŭ*), **128**

Allan, C. W., *Makers of Cathay*, 49 n. 79, **157**

Altai, mountains, I, 35

Altar, for sacrifices, 137

American libraries, *see* Gardner, C. S.

Amiot, "Suite des Vies ou Portraits des célèbres Chinois," 49 n. 79, 74 n. 10, 108 n. 23, **152**

Amnesty, 109, 114

An(-chou), **75**

Anhui, modern province, 17 n. 35, 63, 64, 75 n. 20, 140

Animals, rare, 13

Annam, 155

An-ting(-chün), II–4D, **136**, 140

Aoyama Sadao, author, 16 n. 33, **158**, 159

Archer Guards (*hou-wei*), **129**; General of the Right (*yu-hou-wei chiang-chün*), **132**

Archers, 92. *See also* Bowmen

Archives, 147

Armies (*chün*), **96**; T'ang organization, 96, 97

Articles, legal, (*t'iao*), **108**

Asbestos, 26

Assistant Commandery Administrator (*chün-ch'êng*), **70**, 133, 138

Assistant Supervisor in the Administration of the Imperial Domestic Service (*tien-nei shao-chien*), **76**

Associate Garrison Commander (*fu-liu-shou*), **88** n. 27, 94

Associate General (*fu-chiang*), **88**, 94

Associate Supervisor (*fu-chien*), **85, 87**

Atlases, 157–159

Authorization (*pao*), **93**

Baghatur shad (Mo-ho-tu shê), Hsieh-li Khan, **113**

Ballad, of rise of Li, **51**, 52, 54, 68, 76, 80, 118. *See also* Li

Banditry, *see* Rebellions and banditry. *See also* Robbers and thieves.

Banners, imperial, 19

Banquets, Court of Imperial, (*kuang-lu-ssŭ*), **128**; Vice President of, (*kuang-lu shao-ch'ing*), **138**

Barbarian states, **28**, 92

Barbarians, invaders of North China, 3–5; Hu, **133**; in Ling-nan, 136 n. 8

Barges, imperial, 17, 56, 57

Beasts, hunting of, 19

Bibliography, 145–159; bibliographical aids, 146, 147, 154

Bingham, W., reviews by, 155; "Wên Ta-ya," 83 n. 2, **154**

Biographies, dates determined, xi; basis of investigation, 8, 10; of rebels, 61; Chinese sources, 148; translated, 151; reference works, 157

Wang Tê-jên, **133**
Wang Tzŭ-ying, **138**
Wang Wei, **94**
Wang Yao-han, **140**
War, Board of, (*ping-pu*), **128**; President of, (*ping-pu shang-shu*), **8**
Watches (*fu*), **129**
Water-control, Administration of, (*tu-shui-chien*), **129**; development of public works for, see Chi, C. T.
Wei, see Guards and Guardsmen
Wei Chêng, **148**
Wei Ch'i-lin, **135**
Wei, Duke of, **68**, 138
Wei, northern dynasty, 148
Wei River (Wei-ho or Wei-shui), **15**, navigation on, 16; valley of, 15, 16, 45, 105, 106, 110; headwaters of, 71, 119; T'ang operations near, 103
Wei, Three Kingdoms dynasty, 85
Wei Tao-êrh (or Tiao-êrh), 67 n. 39, **79 n. 45**, 134–136
Wei-fu ta-shih, see Legate Pacifical
Wei-ho, see Wei River
Wei-shih, see Yü-shih
Wei-shui, see Wei River
Wei-wei shao-ch'ing, see Vice President of the Court of Imperial Insignia
Wei-wei-ssŭ, **128**
Wên Ta-ya, x, 49 n. 82, **83**, 84, 97, 120, 122, 149, 154
Wêng Wên-hao, author, **157**
Wên-hsiang, II-5F, **44 n. 48**, 131
Wên-hsien, see Empress Wên-hsien
Wên-têng(-hsien), II-3K, **141**
Wen-ti, see Emperor Wên
West, routes to, 119
West River, 45, 62
Western capital (Hsi-tu), **13**, 70, 71. See also Ch'ang-an
Western Ch'in, King Lord Protector of, (*Hsi Ch'in pa-wang*), **71**, 139
Western Regions (Hsi-yü), 25–31, 56; definition of, **26 n. 15**; geography of, 26 n. 20; Western Turk domination, 35, 36
Western Turks (T'u-chüeh), **33**, 34–36; not part of "Western Regions," 26;

empire of, 35, 36; raid T'u-yü-hun, 45; aid T'ang, 98, 101, 102, 121–123; aid T'ang rival, 106
Wieger, L., *La Chine à travers les âges*, 147; *Textes Historiques*, 2 n. 4, **153**
Wilhelm, R., *Geschichte der Chinesischen Kultur*, **153**
Willows, along canal, 17
Wing Guards (*i-wei*), **129**; Generalissimo of the Left (*tso-i-wei ta-chiang-chün*), **131**
Wo-kuo, see Japan
Works, Administration of, (*chiang-tso-chien*), **129**; Director of, **134**
Workshops, Administration of Imperial, (*shao-fu-chien*), **128**
Wu, region, 62, **131**; King of, **140**
Wu Hai-liu, **131**
Wu Tuan-êrh, **77 n. 36**
Wu(-chün), II-7K, **131**
Wu-pên lang-chiang, see Hu-pên lang-schiang
Wu-t'ai Mountains, E. of Yen-men II-2G, **80**
Wu-tê, reign title, **111 n. 45**, 114, 125
Wu-wei, see Martial Guards
Wu-wei(-chün), I, **106**, 118
Wu-yüan(-chün), II-1D, **71**, 113
Wylie, A., *Notes on Chinese Literature*, **147**

Yanai Wataru, author, **158**
Yang Chao, 126
Yang Chien, see Emperor Wên
Yang Ching-hsiang, **133**
Yang Chün, 126
Yang Chung, family of, 5 n. 17a
Yang Chung-hsü, **134**
Yang Chung-ta, **140**
Yang family (Sui), 5 n. 17a, 154; related to Li (T'ang), 5; hill of, 52
Yang Hao, Sui "Emperor," **112**, 126
Yang Hsüan-kan, **44 n. 42**, 58; rebellion of, 35, 43–45, 51, 52, 56, 59, 67, 76, 116, 117, 124, 131; biography of, 117
Yang I-ch'ên, **132**, 137
Yang Kuang, **1 n. 1**, 6, 7. See also Emperor Yang
Yang Shih-lin, 65 n. 30, **140**

ADDENDA AND CORRIGENDA TO MAPS IIa AND IIb

ADD:

River:	*Lo-shui,*	located at	5-FG
Towns:	Chin-yang,	" "	3-G
	Ch'ien-yüan,	" "	4-D
	Ho-chien-chün,	" "	2-H
	Ho-yang,	" "	4-G
	Pan-chu,	" "	4-G
	T'ung-kuan,	" "	5-E
	Yung,	" "	5-D
Granaries:	Ch'ang-p'ing-ts'ang,	" "	5-F
	Ho-yang-ts'ang,	" "	5-G
	Hsing-lo-ts'ang,	" "	5-G
	Hui-lo-ts'ang,	" "	5-G
	Li-yang-ts'ang,	" "	4-H
	Yung-feng-ts'ang,	" "	5-E

CHANGE TO CORRECT FORMS:

Ch'ang-p'ing-chün,	located at	4-G
Ching-ling-chün,	" "	7-G
P'ing-i-chün,	" "	4-E
P'o-hai-chün,	" "	3-I
Wu-chün,	" "	7-K
Yü-lin-chün,	" "	1-F

On Map IIa the red 13 at Hsüan-ch'eng-chün (7-J) should be (13).